Sentence Composing for High School

Sentence Composing for High School

A Worktext on Sentence Variety and Maturity

Don Killgallon

Boynton/Cook Publishers
Heinemann
Portsmouth, NH

Boynton/Cook Publishers, Inc.

145 Maplewood Ave., Suite 300
Portsmouth, NH 03801

Offices and agents throughout the world

Library of Congress Cataloging-in-Publication Data
Killgallon, Don.
    Sentence composing for high school : a worktext on sentence
  variety and maturity / Donald Killgallon.
        p.   cm.
    Includes bibliographical references (p. 117).
    ISBN 0-86709-428-1
      1. English language—Sentences—Study and teaching (Secondary)
    2. English language—Composition and exercises—Study and
  teaching (Secondary)   3. English language—Sentences—Problems,
  exercises, etc.   I. Title.
    LB1631.K47   1998
    808'.042'0712—dc21   97-39413
                                                                  CIP

Editor: Peter R. Stillman
Production: Elizabeth Valway
Cover Design: Jenny Jensen Greenleaf
Manufacturing: Louise Richardson

Printed in the United States of America on acid-free paper

33 34 35 36 37 VP 25 24 23 22 21

To Bob Boynton:
For the spunk and the savvy that paved the way,
the gentle demurrers that saved the day.

Contents

*P*reface

> When it comes to language, nothing is more satisfying than to write a good sentence.
>
> *—Barbara Tuchman*

This series—*Sentence Composing for Middle School, Sentence Composing for High School,* and *Sentence Composing for College*—emphasizes the most neglected unit of written composition: the sentence. Using four sentence-manipulating techniques—*sentence unscrambling, sentence imitating, sentence combining,* and *sentence expanding*—these books teach students structures they seldom use in their writing but should, and can easily use once they become familiar with them through many examples and practices.

Each book concentrates on such structures, by means of model sentences by professional writers. The rationale is based on the widely accepted mimetic theory of *oral* language acquisition, applied here to *written* language acquisition, in the belief that continual exposure to structures used often by professionals in their sentences will produce attention to, understanding of, and, with practice, normal use of such structures by students in their sentences.

The books are exercises in applied grammar, with the theory and terminology of grammar subordinate to the major goal: composing sentences. The naming of parts and the parsing of sentences, the goals of traditional grammar study, are exercises in dissection. The practices in *Sentence Composing* are exercises in production.

The sentence-manipulating techniques are easily learned. The practices based on them are interesting and challenging, and they can be done by any student. In addition, the teacher can readily give attention to the sentences students compose, with quicker, more constant, and more thorough feedback than with longer compositions.

Since the practices have proved successful for the great majority of students who have used them in all kinds of schools, it is demonstrably true that *Sentence Composing* can work anywhere, in any school, with any student.

DON KILLGALLON
Baltimore, Maryland

*I*ntroduction

How Sentence Composing Works

When you or a professional write, you both choose words and arrange them in sentences, but often with different results: variety and maturity in sentences written by professional writers are much more evident than in sentences written by students. Unlike professional writers, students tend to write sentences similar to sentences they speak.

The big difference in variety and maturity is what this worktext is all about. The idea of *sentence composing* is to bridge that gap, so that your sentences more closely resemble in structure those written by professional writers. Throughout the worktext, you will see how professional writers write their sentences. You will learn and practice writing similar sentences by using four easy-to-learn techniques: *sentence unscrambling*, *sentence imitating*, *sentence combining*, and *sentence expanding*.

You will learn by imitating the pros. Just as you used imitation as a child to learn to speak by imitating experienced speakers like your parents, you can learn to write better sentences by imitating how professional writers use written language.

Nothing in the worktext is difficult to learn. You don't have to know a lot about grammar. You don't have to learn lots of terms. You don't have to study to take tests. But you do have to want to improve the sentences you write. This worktext will show you how.

First you have to learn something, and then you can go out and do it.

Mies van der Rohe

---

*H*ow to Use This Worktext

All practices in this worktext use model sentences written by professional writers. Throughout the worktext you will practice sentence unscrambling, sentence imitating, sentence combining, and sentence expanding to learn to write sentences that have the kind of variety and maturity in the model sentences.

You can learn a lot about writing in general through the practices in this worktext, not just about how professionals write their sentences. Even though you will be working with sentences—the backbone of all writing—you can learn skills that will help you improve any kind of writing: paragraphs, essays, short stories, reports, and research papers.

The References section at the end of the worktext contains the original sentences by professional writers used as models in the practices throughout the worktext. Don't consider them the answers in the back of the book, as in a math textbook.

When you look up the original sentences you may decide that the professionally written sentence is better than yours; if so, study the difference. You may, however, decide that yours is just as good; if so, congratulate yourself. You may even decide that yours is better; in that case, take a bow.

1

Tools for Better Sentences

Here you will learn the skills that professional writers
use to compose sentences. Think of them as tools to build
better sentences.

Skill 1

Appositive Phrase

Identifying the Appositive Phrase

Here's a list of sentences, all written by professional writers, but with some parts deleted.

1. It went away slowly.
2. The land that lay stretched out before him became of vast significance.
3. However, I looked with a mixture of admiration and awe at Peter.
4. That night in the south upstairs chamber Emmett lay in a kind of trance.

Now compare those sentences with the originals. Notice that the additions account for the distinctiveness of the original sentences.

1a. It went away slowly, **the feeling of disappointment that came sharply after the thrill that made his shoulders ache**.
> *Ernest Hemingway, "Big Two-Hearted River: Part I"*

2a. The land that lay stretched out before him became of vast significance, **a place peopled by his fancy with a new race of men sprung from himself**.
> *Sherwood Anderson,* Winesburg, Ohio

3a. However, I looked with a mixture of admiration and awe at Peter, **a boy who could and did imitate a police siren every morning on his way to the showers**.
> *Robert Russell,* To Catch an Angel

4a. That night in the south upstairs chamber, **a hot little room where a full-leafed chinaberry tree shut all the air from the single window**, Emmett lay in a kind of trance.
> *Jessamyn West, "A Time of Learning"*

The **boldface** phrases are appositives, one of the sentence parts that differentiate professional writing from student writing. They're frequently used by professional writers but rarely by students. Appositive phrases are an efficient way to combine related ideas in one sentence.

Characteristics of the Appositive Phrase

Appositives are noun phrases that identify adjacent nouns or pronouns. They can occur as sentence openers, subject-verb splits, or sentence closers. Examples are boldfaced.

Sentence Openers

1. **One of eleven brothers and sisters**, Harriet was a moody, willful child.

   Langston Hughes, "Road to Freedom"

2. **A balding, smooth-faced man**, he could have been anywhere between forty and sixty.

   Harper Lee, To Kill a Mockingbird

3. **A short, round boy of seven**, he took little interest in troublesome things, preferring to remain on good terms with everyone.

   Mildred D. Taylor, Roll of Thunder, Hear My Cry

Subject-Verb Splits

4. Poppa, **a good quiet man**, spent the last hours before our parting moving aimlessly about the yard, keeping to himself and avoiding me.

   Gordon Parks, "My Mother's Dream for Me"

5. A man, **a weary old pensioner with a bald dirty head and a stained brown corduroy waistcoat**, appeared at the door of a small gate lodge.

   Brian Moore, The Lonely Passion of Judith Hearne

6. Van'ka Zhukov, **a boy of nine who had been apprenticed to the shoemaker Alyakhin three months ago**, was staying up that Christmas eve.

Anton Chekhov, "Van'ka"

Sentence Closers

7. The boy looked at them, **big black ugly insects**.

Doris Lessing, African Stories

8. Hour after hour he stood there, silent, motionless, **a shadow carved in ebony and moonlight**.

James V. Marshall, Walkabout

9. He had the appearance of a man who had done a great thing, **something greater than any ordinary man would do**.

John Henrik Clarke, "The Boy Who Painted Christ Black"

Practice 1

Unscrambling

Each scrambled sentence has one or more appositives. Identify them. Then unscramble the sentence parts and write out the sentence, punctuating it correctly. Compare your sentences with the originals on page 117 in the references.

1a.   struggled as usual

b.   she

c.   to maintain her calm, composed, friendly bearing

d.   a sort of mask she wore all over her body

D. H. Lawrence, "The Blind Man"

2a.   an old, bowlegged fellow in a pale-blue sweater

b.   the judge

c.   and was reading over some notes he had taken

d.   had stopped examining the animals

e.   on the back of a dirty envelope

Jessamyn West, "The Lesson"

3a. the tyrannosaur

 b. with huge flaring nostrils

 c. a long snuffling inhalation that fluttered Baselton's trouser legs

 d. gave Baselton a smell

Michael Crichton, The Lost World

4a. talked continually of virginity

 b. the son of a jeweler in Winesburg

 c. one of them

 d. a slender young man with white hands

Sherwood Anderson, Winesburg, Ohio

5a. went over to Tom Willy's saloon

 b. in the late afternoon

 c. Will Henderson

 d. and editor of the *Eagle*

 e. owner

Sherwood Anderson, Winesburg, Ohio

6a. and the jingle of trace chains

 b. was louder

 c. drag of brakes

 d. the sound of the approaching grain teams

 e. thud of big hooves on hard ground.

John Steinbeck, Of Mice and Men

7a. with the butt of a teamster's whip

 b. once Enoch Bentley

 c. old Tom Bentley

 d. struck his father

 e. and the old man seemed likely to die

 f. the older one of the boys

Sherwood Anderson, Winesburg, Ohio

8a.   with devil-may-care eyes and a long humorous nose

  b.   Mr. Mick Malloy

  c.   tall cashier with a dignified face

  d.   a nice sort of fellow

  e.   tall, young secret gambler

  f.   a gentlemanly bank clerk

  g.   became Mr. Malloy

> *Brian Moore,* The Lonely Passion of Judith Hearne

Practice 2

Imitating

Unscramble both lists of sentence parts to make two sentences that imitate the first model. Then, imitate the same model by writing your own sentence. Finally, write imitations of the other models, making all of your sentence parts like those in the model.

Model: Beside the fireplace old Doctor Winter sat, bearded and simple and benign, **historian and physician to the town.**

> *John Steinbeck,* The Moon Is Down

Scrambled Imitations

1a.   president and valedictorian of the senior class

  b.   by the podium

  c.   intelligent and composed and smiling

  d.   scholarly Henrietta stood

2a.   beaming and affectionate and happy

  b.   bride and groom in their finery

  c.   they danced

  d.   under the canopy

Other Models

1. **A tall, rawhide man in an unbuttoned, sagging vest**, he was visibly embarrassed by any furnishings that suggested refinement.

    Conrad Richter, "Early Marriage"

2. His car, **a perfectly maintained 1960 Thunderbird that was his pride and joy**, stood in the driveway.

    Stephen King, Needful Things

3. Sara watched him as he walked, **a small figure for his ten years**, wearing faded blue jeans and a striped knit shirt that was stretched out of shape.

    Betsy Byars, The Summer of the Swans

Practice 3

Combining
Study the model, and then combine the sentences that follow into one sentence that imitates the model. Change the first sentence to resemble the first sentence part of the model, the second sentence to resemble the second sentence part of the model, etc. Compare your sentences to the ones on page 118 in the references. Finally, write your own sentence that imitates the model.

Example

Model: Mr. Cattanzara, **a stocky, bald-headed man who worked in a change booth on an IRT station**, lived on the next block after George's, above a shoe repair store.

Bernard Malamud, "A Summer's Reading"

Sentences to Be Combined

a. This is about Jan Carter.

b. She is an unabashed, suntanned flirt.

c. She had smiled at him in the cafeteria line.

d. She transferred to the department near Tom's.

e. She transferred for a "chance" meeting.

Combination

Jan Carter, **an unabashed, suntanned flirt who had smiled at him in the cafeteria line**, transferred to the department near Tom's, for a "chance" meeting.

Imitation

Tom Zengler, **the slower, more heavy-handed pianist who had studied under Professor Samione for a decade**, performed in the recital hall near Jacob's, with an obvious competitive attitude.

---

1. *Model:* Among the company was a lawyer, **a young man of about twenty-five**.

   Anton Chekhov, "The Bet"

   a. She was near the statue.

   b. She was an obvious tourist.

   c. She was an oriental lady.

   d. She had a Kodak camera.

2. *Model:* Sady Ellison, **the daughter of Long Butt Ellison**, worked as a waitress for Turkey Plott in a defiant and condescending fashion.

   Wayne Kernodle, "Last of the Rugged Individualists"

   a. This is about *Gone with the Wind.*

   b. That is the movie with the most reissues.

   c. It originated as a novel.

   d. The novel was of the old South.

   e. The novel was by someone who was unglamorous.

   f. The someone was also unknown.

   g. The someone was an authoress.

3. *Model:* Captain Bentick was a family man, **a lover of dogs and pink children and Christmas**.

   John Steinbeck, The Moon Is Down

   a. "Missouri" is a casserole.

   b. The casserole is special.

    c. It is a blend of several ingredients.

    d. It has potatoes.

    e. It has tomatoes.

    f. The tomatoes are stewed.

    g. It has hamburger.

4. *Model:* He was close to twenty and had needs with the neighborhood girls, but no money to spend, and he couldn't get more than an occasional few cents because his father was poor, and his sister Sophie, who resembled George, **a tall, bony girl of twenty-three**, earned very little, and what she had she kept for herself.

                Bernard Malamud, "A Summer's Reading"

    a. We were far from our destination.

    b. In addition, we were making good time on the interstate.

    c. But there was no time to squander.

    d. In addition, Dad wouldn't stop more than twice a day.

    e. Although we kids were itchy, he wouldn't stop.

    f. In addition, Mom was the one who kept the peace.

    g. She was a shrewd, gentle arbitrator.

    h. She had Solomon's mind.

    i. She circumvented some flare-ups.

    j. And she did something with those she couldn't circumvent.

    k. She left those to Heaven.

Practice 4

Expanding

At the slash mark, add an appositive phrase. In Part 1, the first few words are provided and the number of words omitted from the original is noted in brackets after the slash mark. Approximate that number. In Part 2, add whatever seems appropriate. Compare your appositive phrases with the originals on page 118.

Part 1

1. Thus, one noontime, coming back from the office lunch downstairs a little earlier than usual, he found her and several of the foreign-family girls, as well as four of the American girls, surrounding Polish Mary, **one of the** / [8], who was explaining in rather a high key how a certain "feller" whom she had met the night before had given her a beaded bag, and for what purpose.

     Theodore Dreiser, An American Tragedy

2. The rest were standing around in hatless, smoky little groups of twos and threes and fours inside the heated waiting room, talking in voices that, almost without exception, sounded collegiately dogmatic, as though each young man, in his strident, conversational turn, was clearing up, once and for all, some highly controversial issue, **one that** / [12].

     J. D. Salinger, Franny and Zooey

3. Out in the distances the fans of windmills twinkled, turning, and about the base of each, about the drink tank, was a speckle of dark dots, **a herd of cattle** / [13].

     Glendon Swarthout, Bless the Beasts and Children

4. Perhaps two or three times a year we would come together at a party, one of those teen-age affairs which last until dawn with singing and dancing and silly games such as "Kiss the Pillow," or "Post Office," **the game which** / [18].

     Henry Miller, Stand Still Like the Hummingbird

Part 2

1. My bed was an army cot, /.

     James Thurber, "The Night the Bed Fell"

2. He, /, had fled because of superior perceptions and knowledge.

     Stephen Crane, The Red Badge of Courage

3. I had hardly any patience with the serious work of life which, not that it stood between me and desire, seemed to me child's play, /.

     James Joyce, "Araby"

4. There was Major Hunter, /, /. (two appositive phrases)

John Steinbeck, The Moon Is Down

Putting the Appositive Phrase to Work

Write sentences containing two appositive phrases that identify two different objects, persons, or places within the same sentence. Each of the two phrases must be at least ten words long.

Example

Elvis Presley, **the famous king of 50s rock and roll who achieved fame overnight**, made his first national appearance on the "Ed Sullivan Show," **a live television music and variety program during which the camera man was given special directions for shooting the Presley performance**.

---

*S*kill 2

Participial Phrase

*I*dentifying the Participial Phrase

Here's a list of sentences, all written by professional writers, but with some parts deleted.

1. We could see the lake and the mountains across the lake on the French side.

2. Sadao had his reward.

3. The sun rose clear and bright.

4. Spencer took half an hour.

Now compare those sentences with the originals. Notice that the additions account for the distinctiveness of the original sentence.

1a. **Sitting up in bed eating breakfast**, we could see the lake and the mountains across the lake on the French side.
Ernest Hemingway, A Farewell to Arms

2a. Sadao, **searching the spot of black in the twilight sea that night**, had his reward.
Pearl S. Buck, "The Enemy"

3a. The sun rose clear and bright, **tinging the foamy crests of the waves with a reddish purple**.
Alexander Dumas, Count of Monte Cristo

4a. Spencer took half an hour, **swimming in one of the pools which was filled with the seasonal rain, waiting for the pursuers to catch up to him**.
Ray Bradbury, The Martian Chronicles

The **boldface** phrases are participles, one of the sentence parts that appears frequently in professional writing, but rarely in student writing. Participial phrases are an efficient way to combine related ideas into one sentence.

Characteristics of the Participial Phrase

Participles describe nouns or pronouns. Present participles always end in *ing*. Past participles usually end in *ed*. In the following example, the nouns or pronouns are underlined, the participles are capitalized, and the rest of the participial phrases are boldfaced.

Present Participles

1. She was quite far from the windows which were to her left, and behind her were a couple of tall bookcases, CONTAINING **all the books of the factory library**.

   John Hersey, Hiroshima

2. Minute fungi overspread the whole exterior, HANGING **in a fine tangled web-work from the eaves**.

   Edgar Allan Poe, "The Fall of the House of Usher"

3. STANDING **there in the middle of the street**, Marty suddenly thought of Halloween, of the winter and snowballs, of the schoolyard.

   Murray Heyert, "The New Kid"

4. Professor Kazan, WEARING **a spotlessly white tropical suit and a wide-brimmed hat**, was the first ashore.

   Arthur C. Clarke, Dolphin Island

5. He walked to the corner of the lot, then back again, STUDYING **the simple terrain as if deciding how best to effect an entry**, FROWNING **and** SCRATCHING **his head**.

   Harper Lee, To Kill a Mockingbird

Past Participles

6. In six months a dozen small towns had been laid down upon the naked planet, FILLED **with sizzling neon tubes and yellow electric bulbs**.

   Ray Bradbury, The Martian Chronicles

7. The <u>tent</u>, ILLUMINED **by candle**, glowed warmly in the midst of the plain.

Jack London, The Call of the Wild

8. ENCHANTED **and** ENTHRALLED, <u>I</u> stopped her constantly for details.

Richard Wright, Black Boy

9. The other shoji slammed open, and UNSEEN, <u>Buntaro</u> stamped away, FOLLOWED **by the guard**.

James Clavell, Shogun

10. Her <u>hair</u>, BRAIDED **and** WRAPPED **around her head**, made an ash-blonde crown.

John Steinbeck, The Grapes of Wrath

Participles can occur as sentence openers, subject-verb splits, or sentence closers. Examples are boldfaced.

Sentence Openers

1. **Whistling**, he let the escalator waft him into the still night air.

Ray Bradbury, Fahrenheit 451

2. **Looking over their own troops**, they saw mixed masses slowly getting into regular form.

Stephen Crane, The Red Badge of Courage

3. **Amazed at the simplicity of it all**, I understood everything as never before.

Alphonse Daudet, "The Last Lesson"

Subject-Verb Splits

4. My father, **cautioning me not to work a horse till he had fed fully**, said I had plenty of time to eat myself.

Lincoln Steffens, "A Boy on Horseback"

5. Eckels, **balanced on the narrow path**, aimed his rifle playfully.

Ray Bradbury, "A Sound of Thunder"

6. The sight of Mick's exploring beam of light, **flashing and flickering through the submarine darkness a few yards away**, reminded him that he was not alone.

Arthur C. Clarke, Dolphin Island

Sentence Closers

7. The entire crowd in the saloon gathered about me now, **urging me to drink**.

Richard Wright, Black Boy

8. She called to him, **excited**.

Daphne du Maurier, "The Birds"

9. The magician patted the hand, **holding it quietly with a thumb on its blue veins, waiting for life to revive**.

T. S. White, Book of Merlyn

Practice 1

Unscrambling
Sometimes the positions of participial phrases within a sentence are interchangeable: the same phrase could occur in any position—sentence opener, subject-verb split, or sentence closer. Sometimes, however, only two of the three positions (or only one of the three) are acceptable; the other positions would result in unacceptable grammar, distorted meaning, or lack of emphasis. The following practice requires you to make the right decision about the positioning of participial phrases.

Unscramble each list of sentence parts three times: first, to produce a sentence with a participial phrase in the sentence opener position; next, in the subject-verb split position; and finally, in the sentence closer position. Classify the use of each position as either acceptable or unacceptable. If two positions are acceptable, or if all three are acceptable, discuss which position you prefer. Punctuate correctly. When you finish, compare your sentences with the originals in the references on page 120.

1a. was waiting on the landing outside

 b. Bernard

 c. wearing a black turtleneck sweater, dirty flannels, and slippers

Brian Moore, The Lonely Passion of Judith Hearne

2a. lost his grip

  b. dropping helplessly straight down toward the far end of the trailer

  c. and fell free

  d. Malcolm

Michael Crichton, The Lost World

3a. coming down the pole

  b. with no control over my movements

  c. had a sense

  d. I

  e. of being whirled violently through the air

Richard E. Byrd, Alone

4a. black

  b. a little house

  c. perched on high piles

  d. in the distance

  e. appeared

Joseph Conrad, "The Lagoon"

5a. screaming and begging to be allowed to go with her mother

  b. when we had made our way downstairs

  c. saw the woman with the lovely complexion

  d. Miss Pilzer

  e. we

Gerda Weissmann Klein, All But My Life

Each of the scrambled sentences that follow contains more than one participial phrase. Unscramble each once to produce the most effective arrangement of the sentence parts. Punctuate correctly. When you finish, compare your sentences with the originals in the references on page 120. Which do you like better?

6a. with the cautious, half-furtive effort of the sightless

b. and thumping his way before him

c. he was a blind beggar

d. carrying the traditional battered cane
   MacKinlay Kantor, "A Man Who Had No Eyes"

7a. all had the look of invalids crawling into the hospital on their last legs

b. the passengers

c. blinking their eyes against the blinding sunlight

d. emerging from the mildewed dimness of the customs sheds
   Katherine Anne Porter, Ship of Fools

8a. and yet knowing no way to avoid it

b. that winter my mother and brother came

c. buying furniture on the installment plan

d. and we set up housekeeping

e. being cheated
   Richard Wright, Black Boy

Practice 2

Imitating
Unscramble both lists of sentence parts to make two sentences that imitate the first model. Then, imitate the same model by writing your own sentence. Finally, write imitations of the other models, making all of your sentence parts like those in the model.

Model: As he ran away into the darkness, they repented of their weakness and ran after him, **swearing** and **throwing sticks and great balls of soft mud at the figure that screamed and ran faster and faster into the darkness.**
Sherwood Anderson, Winesburg, Ohio

Scrambled Imitations

1a. as her arm whirled fast over the egg whites

 b. and stared at it

 c. and expressing confusion and frustration over the third direction in the recipe

 d. her face shifted toward the cookbook

 e. grimacing

 f. that listed and explained more and ever more of the procedure

2a. stretching

 b. that beckoned but hid farther and farther from his reach

 c. after Jo-Jo climbed higher onto the counter

 d. but missing jars and boxes in the rear with bright colors

 e. he pulled on the doors

 f. and looked for the candy

Other Models

1. **Weaving in and out among the rocks**, they carried the bamboo baskets on erect heads, unmindful of the salt water that leaked on their half-dried hair.

   Kim Yong Ik, "The Sea Girl"

2. **Enchanted** and **enthralled**, I stopped her constantly for details.

   Richard Wright, Black Boy

3. The child, **relinquished by the nurse**, rushed across the room and rooted shyly in her mother's dress.

   F. Scott Fitzgerald, The Great Gatsby

4. When the car stopped, he strode rapidly around to where Lenny was sitting, hands pressed against the front of his thermal undershirt, **trying to catch his breath** and **wondering if this was the final cardiac arrest**.

   Stephen King, Needful Things

Practice 3

Combining

Study the model, and then combine the sentences that follow into one sentence that imitates the model. Change the first sentence to resemble the first sentence part of the model, the second sentence to resemble the second sentence part of the model, etc. Compare your sentences to the ones on page 121 in the references. Finally, write your own sentence that imitates the model.

Example

Model: The horse found the entrance to the trail where it left the flat and started up, **stumbling and slipping on the rocks**.

John Steinbeck, "Flight"

Sentences to Be Combined

1. The cycle hit something.

2. It hit a stretch.

3. The stretch was ice.

4. It happened as it rounded the bend.

5. In addition, it slid sideways.

6. Then it was tottering.

7. In addition, then it was veering.

8. It was veering toward the shoulder.

Combination

The cycle hit a stretch of ice as it rounded the bend and slid sideways, **tottering and veering toward the shoulder**.

Imitation

His arm contacted the concrete of the schoolyard after he missed the jump and landed hard, **snapping and breaking at the impact**.

1. *Model:* The sound of monotonous ax blows rang through the forest, and the insects, **nodding upon their perches,** crooned like old women.

   Stephen Crane, The Red Badge of Courage

   a. A pile of new debris was doing something.

   b. It cluttered up the driveway.

   c. In addition, the tenants were gazing at the disgrace.

   d. They watched with heavy hearts.

2. *Model:* He stood there, his coat wet, **holding his wet hat,** and said nothing.

   Ernest Hemingway, A Farewell to Arms

   a. The dog did something.

   b. He sat up.

   c. His mouth was clenching the rolled newspaper.

   d. He was wagging his tail.

   e. In addition, he begged a reward.

3. *Model:* The little shack, the rattling, rotting barn were gray-bitten with sea salt, **beaten by the damp wind until they had taken on the color of the granite hills.**

   John Steinbeck, "Flight"

   a. Something had been done to the upholstered pieces.

   b. Something had been done to the expensive, polished tables.

   c. They had been moved into the huge dining room.

   d. They were covered with endless painter's cloths.

   e. This was done so that they would be protected.

   f. The protection was from the splatterings of paint.

4. *Model:* The strength that had been as a miracle in her body left, and she half-reeled across the floor, **clutching at the back of the chair in which she had spent so many long**

days staring out over the tin roofs into the main street of Winesburg.

Sherwood Anderson, Winesburg, Ohio

a. The meeting had been like something.

b. It had been like a marathon among meetings.

c. The meeting continued.

d. In addition, the leader deliberated about his strategy.

e. He was stalling after the last remarks from the representative.

f. The representative was the one with whom he had planned something.

g. What they had planned were so many emergency ploys focusing upon every conceivable tactic.

h. The tactic was for the suppression of the opposition.

Practice 4

Expanding
At the slash mark, add a participial phrase. In Part 1, the first few words are provided and the number of words omitted from the original is noted in brackets after the slash mark. Approximate that number. In Part 2, add whatever seems appropriate. Compare your participial phrases with the originals on page 121.

Part 1

1. With the core of the reel showing, his heart feeling stopped with excitement, **leaning** / [10], Nick thumbed the reel hard with his left hand.

   Ernest Hemingway, "Big Two-Hearted River"

2. Mrs. Carpenter was putting sun-tan oil on Sybil's shoulders, **spreading** / [10].

   J. D. Salinger, Nine Stories

3. Soon the men began to gather, **surveying** / [3], **speaking** / [7].

4. The *Carpathia* ship's passengers pitched in gallantly to help the survivors of the *Titanic*, providing / [2], lending / [1], sewing / [13].

   Walter Lord, a Night to Remember

Part 2

1. The children crawled over the shelves and into the potato and onion bins, /.

   Maya Angelou, I Know Why the Caged Bird Sings

2. He, /, at once looked over his shoulder at her and, /, signaled that he would meet her.

   Theodore Dreiser, An American Tragedy

3. In the late afternoon, the truck came back, / and /, and there was a layer of dust in the bed, and the hood was covered with dust, and the headlights were obscured with a red flour.

   John Steinbeck, The Grapes of Wrath

4. He stood there, / and /, /.

   Roald Dahl, "Beware of the Dog"

Putting the Participial Phrase to Work

Write a paragraph describing someone doing something—studying, daydreaming, making a touchdown, doing the latest dance, etc. Somewhere within the paragraph include in any order imitations of each of the four model sentences that follow. Make all sentences in the paragraph—not just the three imitations—well written so that the imitations are hidden.

Models

1. Inside the walls, a woman was using an air hose to chase bugs off the pavement, herding them along with little blasts of air.

   Barbara Kingsolver, The Bean Trees

2. Taking the stairs two at a time, he didn't even notice me following behind.

   Olive Anne Burns, Cold Sassy Tree

3. I spent the entire day in a sulk, staring out the window, waiting for the rain to stop. (two participles)

Rosa Guy, The Friends

4. Dismayed by what had happened, he buried his face in his hands and cried.

Mildred D. Taylor, Roll of Thunder, Hear My Cry

Skill 3

Absolute Phrase

Identifying the Absolute Phrase

Here's a list of sentences, all written by professional writers, but with some parts deleted.

1. She returned to her bench.

2. The boy watched.

3. About the bones, ants were ebbing away.

4. Six boys came over the hill half an hour early that afternoon, running hard.

Now compare those sentences with the originals. Notice that the additions account for the distinctiveness of the original sentences.

1a. She returned to her bench, **her face showing all the unhappiness that had suddenly overtaken her**.
     Theodore Dreiser, An American Tragedy

2a. The boy watched, **his eyes bulging in the dark**.
     Edmund Ware, "An Underground Episode"

3a. About the bones, ants were ebbing away, **their pincers full of meat**.
     Doris Lessing, African Stories

4a. Six boys came over the hill half an hour early that afternoon, running hard, **their heads down, their forearms working, their breath whistling**. (three absolutes)
     John Steinbeck, The Red Pony

The **boldface** phrases are absolute phrases, one of the sentence parts that differentiates professional writing from student writing. They're frequently used by professional writers but rarely by students. Absolute phrases are an efficient way to combine related ideas in one sentence.

Characteristics of the Absolute Phrase

Absolutes are sentence parts that describe the rest of the sentence in which they appear. Absolutes are *almost* complete sentences. As a test, you can make *any absolute* a sentence by adding *was* or *were*. Here are the four absolutes from the previous examples, changed into sentences:

1a. Her face **was** showing all the unhappiness that had suddenly overtaken her.

2a. His eyes **were** bulging in the dark.

3a. Their pincers **were** full of meat.

4a. Their heads **were** down. Their forearms **were** working. Their breath **was** whistling.

Another way to identify an absolute is that many absolutes begin with the words *my, his, her, its, our, their* (possessive pronouns). Absolutes can occur as sentence openers, subject-verb splits, or sentence closers. Examples are boldfaced.

Sentence Openers

1. **His hands raw**, he reached a flat place at the top.
    Richard Connell, "The Most Dangerous Game"

2. **Each child carrying his little bag of crackling**, we trod the long road home in the cold winter afternoon.
    Peter Abrahams, Tell Freedom

3. Outside, **his carpetbag in his hand**, he stood for a time in the barnyard.
    Jessamyn West, "A Time of Learning"

Subject-Verb Splits

4. Miss Hearne, **her face burning**, hardly listened to these words.
    Brian Moore, The Lonely Passion of Judith Hearne

5. High in the air, a little figure, **his hands thrust in his short jacket pockets,** stood staring out to sea.

Katherine Mansfield, "The Voyage"

6. An Arab on a motorcycle, **his long robes flying in the wind of his speed**, passed John at such a clip that the spirals of dust from his turnings on the winding road looked like little tornadoes.

Elizabeth Yates, "Standing in Another's Shoes"

Sentence Closers

7. She screamed for Klaus—*shrieked* for him—and Klaus came on the dead run, **his work boots whitened by the half-full pail of milk he had spilled on them**.

Stephen King, "The Two Dead Girls"

8. He walked with a prim strut, swinging out his legs in a half-circle with each step, **his heels biting smartly into the red velvet carpet on the floor**.

Carson McCullers, " The Jockey"

9. Those who had caught sharks had taken them to the shark factory on the other side of the cove where they were hoisted on a block and tackle, **their livers removed, their fins cut off, and their hides skinned out**, and **their flesh cut into strips for salting**. (four closers)

Ernest Hemingway, The Old Man and the Sea

Practice 1

Unscrambling

Each scrambled sentence has one or more absolute phrases. Identify them. Then unscramble the sentence parts and write out the sentence, punctuating it correctly. Compare your sentences with the originals on page 122 in the references.

1a.   while Buck struggled in fury

b.   then the rope tightened mercilessly

c.   and his great chest panting

d.   his tongue lolling out of his mouth
                    Jack London, The Call of the Wild

2a. to light the cigarette

b.   his throat sore

c.   he forgot

d.   his head aching
                    Sinclair Lewis, Cass Timberlane

3a. I

b.   each set upon a carved wooden base

c.   looked across to a lighted case of Chinese design

d.   which held delicate-looking statues

e.   of horses and birds, small vases and bowls
                    Ralph Ellison, Invisible Man

4a. was awake for quite a long time

b.   the moonlight on her face

c.   thinking about things

d.   I

e.   and watching Catherine sleeping
                    Ernest Hemingway, A Farewell to Arms

5a. wherever it settled its weight

b.   The dinosaur ran

c.   its taloned feet clawing damp earth

d.   leaving prints six inches deep

e.   its pelvic bones crushing aside trees and bushes
                    Ray Bradbury, "A Sound of Thunder"

6a. her shoulders drooping a little

b.   her glasses winking in the sunlight

    c.   she was now standing arms akimbo

    d.   her head cocked to one side
                                Harper Lee, To Kill a Mockingbird

7a.   as if he could squeal or laugh out loud

  b.   and then

  c.   his hand in one pocket clutching the money

  d.   he felt

  e.   his feet sinking in the soft nap of the carpet
                              Theodore Dreiser, An American Tragedy

8a.   you could hear the signs and murmurs as the furthest chambers of it died

  b.   closing up forever

  c.   the organs malfunctioning

  d.   everything shutting off

  e.   liquids running a final instant from pocket to sac to spleen
                            Ray Bradbury, "A Sound of Thunder"

Practice 2

Imitating

Unscramble both lists of sentence parts to make two sentences that imitate the first model. Then, imitate the same model by writing your own sentence. Finally, write imitations of the other models, making all of your sentence parts like those in the model.

    Model: The motorcycle on the sidewalk speeded up and skidded obliquely into a plate-glass window, **the front wheel bucking and climbing the brick base beneath the window**.
                            Frank Rooney, "Cyclist's Raid"

Scrambled Imitations

1a.   the other customers rallying and demanding the same reduction in the cost

  b.   one customer in the line spoke out

c. about the unfair price

d. and ranted continuously

2a. and moved quickly

b. one couple heading and leading the rest through the complicated steps

c. into two lines

d. several dancers near the band joined together

Other Models

1. Jumping from the bed, **my feet barely hitting the deerskin rug**, I rushed into Mama's room.
   Mildred D. Taylor, Roll of Thunder, Hear My Cry

2. A seared man, **his charred clothes fuming where the blast had blown out the fire**, rose from the curb.
   Fritz Leiber, "A Bad Day for Sales"

3. I found Aunt Loma sitting at the kitchen table, **her long curly hair still loose and tousled, the dirty breakfast dishes pushed back to clear a space**.
   Olive Ann Burns, Cold Sassy Tree

Practice 3

Combining

Study the model, and then combine the sentences that follow into one sentence that imitates the model. Change the first sentence to resemble the first sentence part of the model, the second sentence to resemble the second sentence part of the model, etc. Compare your sentences to the ones on page 123 in the references. Finally, write your own sentence that imitates the model.

Example

Model: He returned, shuddering, five minutes later, **his arms soaked and red to the elbows**.

Ray Bradbury, "A Sound of Thunder"

Sentences to Be Combined

a. This is about the soldiers.

b. They retreated.

c. They were shivering.

d. This happened two days ago.

e. Their spirits were outraged.

f. In addition, their spirits were crushed.

g. This effect on their spirits was caused by the defeat.

Combination

> The soldiers retreated, shivering, two days ago, **their spirits outraged and crushed by the defeat**.

Imitation

> She left, smiling, a minute before, **her Andrew Wyeth print matted and framed in green**.

---

1. *Model:* The electric train was there waiting, **all the lights on**.
   Ernest Hemingway, A Farewell to Arms

   a. The youngest brother was nearby.

   b. He was resting.

   c. All his work was over.

2. *Model:* As soon as she was well, we went to Southend-on-the-Sea for a holiday, **Mother outfitting us completely with new clothes**.
   Charlie Chaplin, My Autobiography

   a. It happened as soon as it was over.

   b. What happened then was that they pranced around Gracie.

   c. They did their prancing like courtiers.

   d. Paul was wooing her disgustingly.

   e. He wooed her with his stretched smiles.

3. *Model:* Then, very afraid, she shook her head warningly, and touched a finger to her lips and shook her head again, **her eyes pleading with him**.

James Clavell, Shogun

   a. Later, he was so happy.

   b. He held the baby.

   c. He held it soothingly.

   d. In addition, he brought the music box to her.

   e. He wound the toy up.

   f. His voice was singing with it.

4. *Model:* The old woman pointed upwards interrogatively and, on my aunt's nodding, proceeded to toil up the narrow staircase before us, **her bowed head being scarcely above the level of the banister-rail**.

James Joyce, "The Sisters"

   a. The student teacher erased everything quickly.

   b. In addition, she did something with a hurried cover-up.

   c. She started to call out the spelling words.

   d. She did this for us.

   e. Her embarrassment was definitely coming from something.

   f. It was coming from her misspelling.

   g. The misspelling was on the chalkboard.

Practice 4

Expanding

At the slash mark, add an absolute phrase. In Part 1, the first few words are provided, and the number of words omitted from the original is noted after the slash mark. Approximate that number. In Part 2, add whatever seems appropriate. Compare your absolute phrases with the originals on page 123.

Part 1

1. Now, in the waning daylight, he turned into Glover Street toward his home, **his arms** / [8].

   Norman Katkov, "The Torn Invitation"

2. As they drove off, Wilson saw her standing under the big tree, looking pretty rather than beautiful in her faintly rosy khaki, **her dark hair** / [14], **her face** / [10].

   Ernest Hemingway,
   "The Short Happy Life of Francis Macomber"

3. His great chest was low to the ground, **his head** [3], **his feet** / [3], **the claws** / [8].

   Jack London, The Call of the Wild

4. In front of the house where we lived, the mountain went down steeply to the little plain along the lake, and we sat on the porch of the house in the sun and saw the winding of the road down the mountain-side and the terraced vineyards on the side of the lower mountain, **the vines** / [6] and **the fields** / [4], and below the vineyards, **the houses** / [11].

   Ernest Hemingway, A Farewell to Arms

Part 2

1. He began scrambling up the wooden pegs nailed to the side of the tree, /.

   John Knowles, A Separate Peace

2. Touser roused himself under Fowler's desk and scratched another flea, /.

   Clifford D. Simak, "Desertion"

3. They were smiling, /, /.

   Jack Finney, "Of Missing Persons"

4. Men, /, /, swung by; a few women all muffled scurried along; and one tiny boy, /, was jerked along angrily between his father and mother; he looked like a baby fly that had fallen into the cream.

   Katherine Mansfield, "The Voyage"

Putting the Absolute Phrase to Work

The paragraph that follows, taken from "All Gold Canon" by Jack London, narrates the shooting and death of a gold miner. At the place indicated within London's paragraph, a sentence has been removed. In that place, write a long sentence describing the miner falling to the ground. Use a series of three consecutive absolutes as part of that description. You are London's partner, with London writing most of the paragraph but you adding a very important part. Make sure your sentence blends smoothly with his paragraph.

Paragraph

> While he debated, a loud, crashing noise burst on his ear. At the same instant he received a stunning blow on the left side of the back, and from the point of impact felt a rush of flame through his flesh. He sprang up in the air, but halfway there his feet collapsed. **[INSERT YOUR SENTENCE HERE.]** His legs twitched convulsively several times. There was a slow expansion of the lungs, accompanied by a deep sigh. Then the air was slowly, very slowly, exhaled, and his body slowly flattened itself down into inertness.

Skill 4

Prepositional Phrase

Identifying the Prepositional Phrase

Here's a list of sentences, all written by professional writers, but with some parts deleted.

1. All children grow up.

2. Lincoln International Airport was functioning.

3. They have no memory.

4. He groped out and began to sob.

Now compare those sentences with the originals. Notice that the additions account for the distinctiveness of the original sentences.

1a.   All children, **except one**, grow up.
J. M. Barrie, Peter Pan

2a.   **At half-past six on a Friday evening in January**, Lincoln International Airport was functioning, **with difficulty**.
Arthur Hailey, Airport

3a.   They have no memory, **of tears or laughter, of sorrow or loving kindness**.
Lloyd Alexander, The Book of Three

4a.   He groped out **for me with both of his own arms, like a drowning man**, and began to sob **against my stomach**.
Stephen King, "The Mouse on the Mile"

The boldface parts are prepositional phrases, another of the sentence parts that differentiate professional writing from student writing. Professional writers sometimes open their sentences with one or more prepositional phrases, use prepositional phrases in a series, and use them in ways most students don't, as you'll see in the practices that follow.

Characteristics of the Prepositional Phrase

Prepositional phrases are sentence parts that describe people, things, or actions. Most begin with one of these prepositions: _in_ the beginning, _before_ the fall, _after_ the creation, _at_ the game, _down_ the aisle, _across_ the street, _inside_ the stadium, _outside_ the store, _between_ the posts, _within_ the den, _behind_ the scenes, _on_ the bridge, _by_ the sea, _under_ the boardwalk, _around_ the park, _down_ the road, _into_ the woods, _against_ the grain, _near_ the field, _through_ the woods, _to_ Grandmother's house, _like_ a bird, _except_ the sophomores, _over_ the rainbow, _up_ the creek, _without_ a paddle, _with_ malice, _toward_ none, _of_ the people, _by_ the people, _for_ the people. Most prepositions are easy to identify because they are difficult to define. (Try defining _of, in, off, by, through, between,_ and so on.) Sentences can contain single or consecutive prepositional phrases anywhere in the sentence.

Single Prepositional Phrases

1. _**In**_ **that place**, the wind prevailed.
    Glendon Swarthout, Bless the Beasts and Children

2. _**At**_ **the bottom**, he looked glumly _**down**_ **the tunnel**.
    Stephen King, "Night Journey"

3. _**With**_ **a quick, guilty hand**, she covered the tear, her shoulders bunching to hide her face.
    Zenna Henderson, The Believing Child

Consecutive Prepositional Phrases

4. _**In**_ **a hole** _**in**_ **the ground**, there lived a hobbit.
    J. R. R. Tolkien, The Hobbit

5. _**Across**_ **the street** _**from**_ **their house,** _**in**_ **an empty lot** _**between**_ **two houses**, stood the rock pile.
    James Baldwin, "Going to Meet the Man"

6. *In* the shade *of* the house, *in* the sunshine *on* the river bank *by* the boats, *in* the shade of the sallow wood and the fig tree, Siddhartha, the handsome Brahmin's son, grew up.

Hermann Hesse, Siddhartha

Prepositional phrases can occur as sentence openers, subject-verb splits, or sentence closers. Examples are boldfaced, with the prepositions also placed in italics.

Sentence Openers

1. *Like* a lean, gray wolf, he moved silently and easily.

Lloyd Alexander, The Book of Three

2. *Through* the fence, *between* the curling flower spaces, I could see them hitting.

William Faulkner, The Sound and the Fury

Subject-Verb Splits

3. Ancestors, *in* every variety of dress, *from* the Elizabethan knight *to* the buck *of* the Regency, stared down and daunted us.

Arthur Conan Doyle, The Hound of the Baskervilles

4. Bearded men, *in* sad-colored garments and gray, steeple-crowned hats, intermixed with women.

Nathaniel Hawthorne, The Scarlet Letter

Sentence Closers

5. The sea is high again today, *with* a thrilling flush *of* wind.

Lawrence Durrell, Justine

6. Then they came, *up* the street and *around* the house.

Hal Borland, When the Legends Die

Practice 1

Unscrambling

Each scrambled sentence has one or more prepositional phrases. Identify them. Then unscramble the sentence parts and write out the sentence, punctuating it correctly. Compare your sentences with the originals on page 125 in the references.

1a.   across the ripples

 b.   it was morning

 c.   and the new sun sparkled gold

 d.   of a gentle sea
                    Richard Bach, Jonathan Livingston Seagull

2a.   the boy felt good

 b.   in his mouth

 c.   of ham and biscuit

 d.   with the flavor
                         William H. Armstrong, Sounder

3a.   and neither knew

 b.   for the first fifteen years

 c.   Danny and I lived

 d.   of our lives

 e.   within five blocks of each other

 f.   of the other's existence
                              Chaim Potok, The Chosen

4a.   and grabbed Coffey's slab

 b.   at that moment

 c.   between the bars

 d.   a skinny arm shot out

 e.   of a bicep

 f.   of Wharton's cell
                         Stephen King, "Night Journey"

5a.   by a hundred bees

 b.   his face felt

 c.   by the end

d.   as if it had been stung

e.   of the first round

Robert Lipsyte, The Contender

6a.   I could see the doctor

b.   with his black bag

c.   over Dean's shoulder

d.   between his feet

e.   against the wall

Stephen King, "Coffey on the Mile"

7a.   making one big pile and three smaller ones

b.   Ima Dean

c.   delving into it

d.   of yellow and red wrapped candies

e.   on the floor

f.   with a huge bag

g.   was sitting

Bill and Vera Cleaver, Where the Lilies Bloom

8a.   in one

b.   with the ivy behind her

c.   of Colin's books

d.   she was

e.   and with her nice fresh face smiling across the greenery

f.   with the sunlight through the trees

g.   dappling her long blue cloak

h.   like a softly colored illustration

Frances Hodgson Burnett, The Secret Garden

Practice 2

Imitating

Unscramble both lists of sentence parts to make two sentences that imitate the first model. Then, imitate the same model by writing your own sentence. Finally, write imitations of the other models, making all of your sentence parts like those in the model.

Model: The aftermath of the shooting was a three-ring circus, *with* the governor in one ring, *with* the prison in another, and *with* poor brain-blasted Percy Wetmore in the third.

Stephen King, The Green Mile

Scrambled Imitations

1a. *near* the canal by the old barn

 b. is a mile from the interstate

 c. the nature trail

 d. and *near* the old abandoned post office across from the church on Front Street

 e. *near* the historic museum in the 19th-century village

2a. and *in* the main office with stressed-out administrators in high demand but low supply

 b. *in* the guidance department with countless schedule changes

 c. was chaos

 d. *in* the cafeteria with huge lines

 e. the first day of classes

Other Models

1. *Across* the stark land, *into* the pine woods, *into* the brightening glow *of* the dawn, the boy followed the dog, whose anxious pace slowed *from* age as they went.

William H. Armstrong, Sounder

2. One man had died, but now the remaining sixteen, *with* their eyes clear *in* their heads and their faces pressed *to* the thick glass ports, watched Mars swing up *under* them.

Ray Bradbury, The Martian Chronicles

3. When the *Titanic* brushed the iceberg, several tons *of* ice crumbled *off* the berg and landed *on* the starboard well deck, *opposite* the foremast.

Walter Lord, A Night to Remember

Practice 3

Combining

Study the model, and then combine the sentences that follow into one sentence that imitates the model. Change the first sentence to resemble the first sentence part of the model, the second sentence to resemble the second sentence part of the model, etc. Compare your sentences to the ones on page 126 in the references. Finally, write your own sentence that imitates the model.

Example

Model: **Without** a pause, I rushed up *to* the east window and scrambled *down* the wall, as I had done before, *into* the Count's room.

Bram Stoker, Dracula

Sentences to Be Combined

a. He did something in a hurry.

b. He ran down to the cafeteria and got into the line.

c. He did this as he had done daily.

d. The line he got into was for fast food.

Combination

In **a hurry,** he ran down *to* **the cafeteria** and got *into* **the line,** as he had done daily, *for* **fast food.**

Imitation

Without **a single thought,** Jack started his car *in* **a flash** and backed *out* **the driveway,** as he did all the time, *into* **the street.**

1. *Model:* **On the boards *of* both the porch and the steps beyond the mutilated screen door**, there were spatters *of* blood.

   Stephen King, "Two Dead Girls"

   a. Something happened under the hood of the truck.

   b. Something also happened within the interior of the cabin.

   c. What happened was that there were wisps.

   d. The wisps were of smoke.

2. *Model:* **With the silence and immobility *of* a great reddish-tinted rock**, Thor stood for many minutes, looking out *over* **his domain**.

   James Oliver Curwood, The Grizzly King

   a. Something happened from the rain.

   b. It also happened from the wind of the most fierce hurricane.

   c. What happened was that the crops drooped.

   d. They drooped toward the soil.

   e. They were drying out from the sun.

3. *Model:* **Around quitting time**, Tod Hackett heard a great din *in* **the road *outside*** his office.

   Nathaniel West, The Day of the Locust

   a. It happened during the ninth inning.

   b. What happened was that Sherman caught a fly ball.

   c. He caught it in the left field.

   d. He caught it near the fence.

4. *Model:* **Into the darkening sky**, unearthly humps of land curved *like* **the backs of browsing pigs, *like* the rumps of elephants**.

   Enid Bagnold, National Velvet

   a. Something happened on the Internet.

   b. What happened was that vast amounts of data traveled.

    c. The data traveled with the speed of invisible light.

    d. The data traveled with clear resolution of graphics.

Practice 4

Expanding

At the slash mark, add a prepositional phrase. In Part 1, the preposition is provided and the number of words omitted from the original is noted after the slash mark. Approximate that number. In Part 2, add whatever seems appropriate. Compare your prepositional phrases with the originals on page 126.

Part 1

1. *On* / [2], gulls woke.

Esther Forbes, Johnny Tremain

2. Dad was a tall man *with* / [9].

Ernestine and Frank Gilbreth, Cheaper by the Dozen

3. The crowd chased us *under* / [3], *around* / [2], *up* [1], *around* / [1], *down* / [1], *into* / [3].

Daniel Keyes, "Flowers for Algernon"

4. Then he talked *of* / [2], *of* / [1], **of** / [6], **of** / [6].

James Hilton, Goodbye, Mr. Chips

Part 2

5. /, they went home.

Ray Bradbury, The Martian Chronicles

6. The snow deadened his careful footsteps, /, / /.

Robert Lipsyte, The Contender

7. He went the back way, /, /, and / .

Harper Lee, To Kill a Mockingbird

8. Then, / , / , the shark plowed / as a speedboat does.

Ernest Hemingway, The Old Man and the Sea

Putting the Prepositional Phrase to Work

Edgar Allan Poe's famous opening sentence for "The Fall of the House of Usher" depends on prepositional phrases for its power.

Here are two versions, one without, and one with, prepositional phrases. Notice how the prepositional phrases improve the style and the content.

Without Prepositional Phrases

> When the clouds hung oppressively low, I had been passing alone and found myself, as the shades drew on.

With Prepositional Phrases

> During the whole of a dull, dark, and soundless day in the autumn of the year, when the clouds hung oppressively low in the heavens, I had been passing alone, on horseback, through a singularly dreary tract of country; and at length found myself, as the shades of evening drew on, within view of the melancholy House of Usher.

Prepositional phrases have been removed from the following opening sentences of famous stories. Add several to each sentence for descriptive power and maturity of style. Finally, check the references on page 127 to see the original sentences.

1. A man stood, looking down twenty feet below.
    Ambrose Bierce, "An Occurrence at Owl Creek Bridge"

2. A man traveling entered the little town.
    Victor Hugo, Les Miserables

3. The boy lowered himself and began to pick his way.
    William Golding, Lord of the Flies

4. A boy was born.
    Mark Twain, The Prince and the Pauper

Note: The sentence from Dickens is a series of contrasting pairs. Each phrase has two words: the preposition *of* plus another word. The first pair is an example.

5. It was the best *of* **times**, it was the worst *of* **times**, it was the age *of* . . . , it was the age *of* . . . , it was the epoch *of* . . . , it was the epoch *of* . . . , it was the season *of* . . . , it was the season *of* . . . , it was the spring *of* . . . , it was the winter *of* . . . .
    Charles Dickens, A Tale of Two Cities

Skill 5

Adjective Clause

*I*dentifying the Adjective Clause

Here's a list of sentences, all written by professional writers, but with some parts deleted.

1. I used to have a cat, an old fighting tom.

2. She lived in a small frame house with her invalid mother and a thin, sallow, unflagging aunt.

3. That spirit of discord was gone.

4. Louise tried to make talk, but the country boy was embarrassed and would say nothing.

Now compare those sentences with the originals. Notice that the additions account for the distinctiveness of the original sentences.

1a. I used to have a cat, an old fighting tom, **who would jump through the open window by my bed in the middle of the night and land on my chest**.
   Annie Dillard, Pilgrim at Tinker Creek

2a. She lived in a small frame house with her invalid mother and a thin, sallow, unflagging aunt, **where each morning between ten and eleven she would appear on the porch in a lace-trimmed boudoir cap to sit swinging in the porch swing until noon**.
   William Faulkner, "Dry September"

3a. That spirit of discord, **which had jumbled my thoughts like powerful fingers sifting through sand or grains of rice**, was gone.
   Stephen King, "Night Journey"

4a.   Louise, **whose mind was filled with thoughts of him**,
      tried to make talk, but the country boy was embarrassed
      and would say nothing.

Sherwood Anderson, Winesburg, Ohio

   The boldface parts are adjective clauses, another of the
sentence parts that differentiate professional writing from
student writing. They're frequently used by professional writers
but rarely by students. Adjective clauses are an efficient way to
combine related ideas in one sentence.

Characteristics of the Adjective Clause

Adjective clauses are sentence parts that describe whatever is
mentioned to the left of them in the same sentence. Most begin
with the words: *who*, *which*, *whose*, or *where*. They can occur as
subject-verb splits, or sentence closers. Examples are boldfaced.

Subject-Verb Splits

1. Keeton, ***who* overtopped Norris by five inches and
   outweighed him by a hundred pounds**, gave the deputy
   a harsh little shake and then did let go.

Stephen King, Needful Things

2. Even his eyes, ***which* had been young**, looked old.

John Steinbeck, The Red Pony

3. His face, ***whose* shades we had often labeled**, now
   achieved a new one.

John Knowles, A Separate Peace

Sentence Closers

4. They dropped his belongings at the freshman dorm, ***where*
   the only sign of his roommate was a khaki duffel bag
   and a canvas butterfly chair printed to resemble a
   gigantic hand**.

Anne Tyler, Saint Maybe

5. I loved school with a desperate passion, ***which* became
   more intense when I began to realize what a**

monumental struggle it was for my parents and brothers and sisters to keep me there.

Eugenia Collier, "Sweet Potato Pie"

6. I began to wonder what God thought about Westley, ***who*** **certainly hadn't seen Jesus either**, but ***who* was now sitting proudly on the platform swinging his knickerbockered legs and grinning down at me**. (two closers)

Langston Hughes, The Big Sea

Practice 1

Unscrambling

Each scrambled sentence has one or more adjective clauses. Identify them. Then unscramble the sentence parts and write out the sentence, punctuating it correctly. Compare your sentences with the originals on page 127 in the references.

1a. a pretty good light-heavyweight

  b. there was one fighter in those days

  c. named Junior Ellis

  d. before a bout

  e. who used to sing along with country and western records

Robert Lipsyte, The Contender

2a. whose eyes were quicker than most

  b. Little Jon

  c. on the stars

  d. should have seen the hole

  e. but all his attention was

Alexander Key, The Forgotten Door

3a. peering from a distance at Jem

  b. to a corner

  c. Boo had drifted

    d.   of the room

    e.   where he stood with his chin up
> *Harper Lee,* To Kill a Mockingbird

4a.   as the probable liberal candidate for Mid-Devon

    b.   the recent sudden death of Sir Charles Baskerville

    c.   has cast a gloom over the county

    d.   at the next election

    e.   whose name has been mentioned
> *Sir Arthur Conan Doyle,* The Hound of the Baskervilles

5a.   after the night's tides

    b.   bare-legged to the beach

    c.   which lies smooth, flat, and glistening

    d.   we run

    e.   with fresh wet shells
> *Anne Morrow Lindbergh,* Gift from the Sea

6a.   who defied authority for the sake of defiance

    b.   whose word was law among boys

    c.   this leader

    d.   and looked even younger

    e.   was no more than twelve or thirteen years old
> *Henry Gregor Felsen,* "Horatio"

7a.   in pursuit of him

    b.   Philippe had dashed

    c.   thinking that his brother had run away with Christine

    d.   where he knew that everything was prepared for the elopement

    e.   along the Brussels Road
> *Gaston Leroux,* The Phantom of the Opera

8a. that people of honest feeling and sensibility

 b. born with low intelligence

 c. how strange it is

 d. born without arms or legs or eyes

 e. who would not take advantage of a man

 f.   think nothing of abusing a man
Daniel Keyes, "Flowers for Algernon"

Practice 2

Imitating
Unscramble both lists of sentence parts to make two sentences that imitate the first model. Then, imitate the same model by writing your own sentence. Finally, write imitations of the other models, making all of your sentence parts like those in the model.

Model: I left the cell, turned the locks, then faced Delacroix, ***who* was standing across the way with his hands wrapped around the bars of his cell**, looking at me anxiously.
Stephen King, "Coffey's Hands"

Scrambled Imitations

1a. making his daily rounds

 b. then greeted the mailman

 c. who was going down the street with his mailbag over his shoulder

 d. I closed the door, went outside

2a. who was rehearsing with only a piano for accompaniment

 b. the producer entered the theatre, took a seat

 c. learning the choreography

 d. then watched the dancer

Other Models

1. Thoroughly frightened, she telephoned Mr. Link at his store, **which was not too far from his house**.

    Harper Lee, To Kill a Mockingbird

2. Mr. Posey, **who was close to tears by now**, told the truth.

    Jean Merrill, The Pushcart War

3. One day in the early summer Squealer ordered the sheep to follow him, and led them out to a piece of waste ground at the other end of the farm, **which had become overgrown with birch saplings**.

    George Orwell, Animal Farm

4. He started to wrap the other end of the wire around the antenna, but his fingers, **which had moved with rapid surety at first**, began to slow down.

    Stephen King, Needful Things

Practice 3

Combining
Study the model, and then combine the sentences that follow into one sentence that imitates the model. Change the first sentence to resemble the first sentence part of the model, the second sentence to resemble the second sentence part of the model, etc. Compare your sentences to the ones on page 128 in the references. Finally, write your own sentence that imitates the model.

Example

> *Model*: The lowest step, **where the stream collected before it tumbled down a hundred feet and disappeared into the rubbly desert**, was a little platform of stone and sand.
>
> *John Steinbeck,* The Pearl

Sentences to Be Combined

a. This is about the parking lot.

b. It is where the students gathered.

c. They gathered there after the game ended in overtime.

d. And the game then brought a close victory.

e. The victory was for the home team.

f. The parking lot was a mass of shouts and cheers.

Combination

The parking lot, ***where* the students gathered after the game ended in overtime and then brought a close victory for the home team**, was a mass of shouts and cheers.

Imitation

The computer lab, ***where* the hackers assembled when the computer contest began and competed with intensity**, resounded with rapid clicks on keyboards.

---

1. *Model:* Jumping to his feet and breaking off the tale, Doctor Parcival began to walk up and down in the office of the *Winesburg Eagle*, ***where* George Willard sat listening**.

    Sherwood Anderson, Winesburg, Ohio

    a. It happened as he was walking in his boots and sinking into mud.

    b. The landscaper started to inspect the front of the garden.

    c. In addition, he started to inspect the back of the garden.

    d. In both places the downpour had washed away things.

    e. What it washed away was many of the new plants.

2. *Model:* After standing still for a moment, as if to observe the sick woman from a little distance, he crossed to the bed, ***which* was illuminated by a single bedside lamp**.

    Stephen King, "Night Journey"

    a. It happened while scrutinizing lovingly from the hallway.

    b. The scrutinizing was as if to rearrange all the china and flowers for the bridal party.

c. What happened was she walked toward the dining table.

d. It was the table which was covered by something.

e. It was covered by a pure white lace tablecloth.

3. *Model:* Dorothy lived in the midst of the great Kansas prairies, with Uncle Henry, **who was a farmer**, and Aunt Em, **who was the farmer's wife**.

   L. F. Baum, The Wizard of Oz

   a. Meredith perched in her apartment loft.

   b. The loft was in the bohemian district.

   c. Meredith was with Tramp, who was a mutt.

   d. In addition, Meredith was with Lady, who was a blue-ribbon pedigree.

4. *Model:* They had planned to spend the first night at Bardstown, **which in good weather was only a few hours away**, and **where there was an attractive old inn**.

   Peter Taylor, "Reservations: A Love Story"

   a. They had stopped to relax that afternoon.

   b. The place they stopped was at Berkeley Springs.

   c. Berkeley Springs was the place which on most days was a very popular tourist site.

   d. In addition, Berkeley Springs was the place where there was a famous spring-water well.

Practice 4

Expanding
At the slash mark, add an adjective clause. In Part 1, the first few words are provided and the number of words that were omitted from the original is noted after the slash mark. Approximate that number. In Part 2, add whatever seems appropriate. Compare your adjective clauses with the originals on page 129.

Part 1

1. Before Sheila left for America to be married two years before, she gave Ma a large and very beautiful volume of the complete works of Shakespeare, **which** is / [4].

   Christy Brown, My Left Foot

2. His black hair, **which** had been / [6], was dry now and blowing.

   J. D. Salinger, "The Laughing Man"

3. Percy had returned to the storage room, **where** he probably / [8].

   Stephen King, "Night Journey"

4. The women, **who** were never [13], now must take the place of the men and face the dangers that abound beyond the village.

   Scott O'Dell, Island of the Blue Dolphins

Part 2

5. Mr. Sherlock Holmes, /, was seated at the breakfast table.

   Sir Arthur Conan Doyle, The Hound of the Baskervilles

6. The terror, /, began, so far as I know or can tell, with a boat made from a sheet of newspaper floating down a gutter swollen with rain.

   Stephen King, It

7. The taxi driver, /, carefully placed Miss Hearne in the back seat of his car and started the engine.

   Brian Moore, The Lonely Passion of Judith Hearne

8. One evening in late fall, George ran out of his house to the library, /.

   Bernard Malamud, "A Summer's Reading"

Putting the Adjective Clause to Work

Add detail to the paragraph below by writing an adjective clause to describe any four underlined words. Use each of these words once to begin the clause: *who, which, whose, where.*

Paragraph to Expand

Trying to figure out the <u>problem</u>, the computer <u>technician</u> sat down in front of the <u>computer</u>. A college freshman employed by the university part-time, in high school she had earned the highest award for expertise in <u>computer technology</u>. Sitting now in front of the computer screen, she thought the problem was probably in the <u>guts of the computer</u>. Removing the <u>case</u>, she looked at the connections on the logic board, the main part of the computer. She spotted the problem instantly, and got up to go to the <u>supply room</u>. She requisitioned the part from the <u>clerk</u>.

Skill 6

Adverb Clause

Identifying the Adverb Clause

Here's a list of sentences, all written by professional writers, but with some parts deleted.

1. He ate.

2. I was just fourteen years of age.

3. The number thirteen proved unlucky for Harry Cone and his crew of twelve aboard the big PBM.

4. Shrinking is always more painful than growing, but the pain was over quickly enough.

Now compare those sentences with the originals. Notice that the additions account for the distinctiveness of the original sentences.

1a.   He ate **while his blanket, still damp, steamed in front of the fire**.

Hal Borland, When the Legends Die

2a.   I was just fourteen years of age **when a coward going by the name of Tom Chaney shot my father down in Fort Smith, Arkansas, and robbed him of his life and his horse and $150 in cash money plus two California gold pieces that he carried in his trouser band**.

Charles Portis, True Grit

3a.   The number thirteen proved unlucky for Harry Cone and his crew of twelve aboard the big PBM, **for the giant plane was never heard from again**.

Richard Winer, The Devil's Triangle

4a.   Shrinking is always more painful than growing, **since for a moment all your bones jam together like a crowd**

on market day, but the pain was over quickly enough as I became the size of a cat.

Laurence Yep, Dragonwings

The boldface parts are adverb clauses, another of the sentence parts that differentiate professional writing from student writing.

Characteristics of the Adverb Clause

Adverb clauses are sentence parts that tell more about the rest of the sentence in which they appear. They usually tell *why, how, when,* or *under what condition* something was done. Most begin with the words *after, if, because, although, when, as, before, until, for,* or *since* (subordinators). They can occur as sentence openers, subject-verb splits, or sentence closers. Examples here are boldfaced, with the subordinator also in italics.

Sentence Openers

1. *After* **he got himself under control**, he apologized. (Tells when he apologized.)

   Stephen King, "The Mouse on the Mile"

2. *If* **you know whence you came**, there is really no limit to where you can go. (Tells the condition for not having limits.)

   James Baldwin, "Letter to My Nephew"

3. *Because* **its primary reason for existence was government**, Maycomb was spared the grubbiness that distinguished most Alabama towns its size. (Tells why Maycomb wasn't grubby.)

   Harper Lee, To Kill a Mockingbird

4. *Although* **they lived in style**, they felt always an anxiety in the house. (Tells an ironic condition.)

   D. H. Lawrence, "The Rocking-Horse Winner"

Subject-Verb Splits

5. The truck drivers, *when* **they heard that Maxie Hammerman had been released**, were furious. (Tells when the drivers were furious.)

   Jean Merrill, The Pushcart War

6. Uncle Hammer, *as* **he had every day since he had arrived**, wore sharply creased pants, a vest over a snow-white shirt, and shoes that shone like midnight. (Tells when he dressed neatly.)

   Mildred D. Taylor, Roll of Thunder, Hear My Cry

7. Raisl, *before* **they were married**, had made the bag out of a piece of her dress and embroidered it with the tablets of the Ten Commandments. (Tells when Raisl made the bag.)

   Bernard Malamud, The Fixer

Sentence Closers

8. Alfred quietly slipped out the back door and waited *until* **Henry left.** (Tells when Alfred waited.)

   Robert Lipsyte, The Contender

9. Bert seemed a little sheepish *as* **he followed the other members to their seats at the front of the room.** (Tells when Bert seemed sheepish.)

   John Steinbeck, The Red Pony

10. A pile of silver coins grew at the door flap *when* **a baby died,** *because* **a baby must be well buried,** *since* **it has had nothing else of life.** (Contains three closers. The first adverb clause tells when people give money to the parents of a baby who has died; the next two tell why.)

    John Steinbeck, The Grapes of Wrath

Practice 1

Unscrambling

Each scrambled sentence has one or more adverb clauses. Identify them. Then unscramble the sentence parts and write out the sentence, punctuating it correctly. Compare your sentences with the originals on page 129–130 in the references.

1a. like a shot

 b. tears streaming

 c. was out of the control room

    d.   when it was over

    e.   Susan

                                       Anonymous, Primary Colors

2a. and rubbed his swollen ankle

    b.   finally

    c.   while he gained his breath

    d.   removed one boot

    e.   he huddled by a fallen log

                              Alexander Key, The Forgotten Door

3a. distributing his bundle of papers

    b.   when he got back into town

    c.   before he went home to supper

    d.   he would have to go on

                  Sherwood Anderson, "Death in the Woods"

4a. and listened to the fire crack

    b.   while he put the food in his mouth and chewed thoughtfully

    c.   when the sun set

    d.   and cooked a small supper

    e.   he crouched by the path

                    Ray Bradbury, The Martian Chronicles

5a. took a hammer with a homemade handle

    b.   when kernel-picking time came

    c.   the boy or the father

    d.   and cracked as many walnuts as could be kerneled in a night

    e.   went to the flat rock

    f.   before it was dark each day

                    William H. Armstrong, Sounder

6a.   stuck into a white mess of bread dough

b.   her face

c.   and her eyes

d.   as she stepped into the light

e.   was round and thick

f.   were like two immense eggs
         Ray Bradbury, The Martian Chronicles

7a.   although oil had kept off the frost so far

b.   when the seal was dead

c.   before it could freeze

d.   getting rid of the wet from her coat

e.   the bear attended first to herself
         Norah Burke, "Polar Night"

8a.   who begged for food and shelter

b.   ragged, hungry, and footsore

c.   one autumn night

d.   and opening it

e.   when the first heavy rains were falling and a cold wind
      whistled through the valley

f.   a knock came at the minister's door

g.   he found an Indian boy
         Louisa May Alcott, "Onawandah"

Practice 2

Imitating
Unscramble both lists of sentence parts to make two sentences
that imitate the first model. Then, imitate the same model by
writing your own sentence. Finally, write imitations of the other
models, making all of your sentence parts like those in the
model.

Model: **As she approached the top of the ridge**, she came to a game trail, a wide muddy track through the jungle.

Michael Crichton, The Lost World

Scrambled Imitations

1a.   the best left hand in professional basketball

  b.   he slam-dunked with his left hand

  c.   after he jumped toward the edge of the rim

2a.   she walked away with the trophy for first place

  b.   a golden statue in the shape of a piano

  c.   although she had the fewest years of piano lessons among the contestants

Other Models

1. ***After* Billy left him and walked angrily away**, Jody turned up toward the house.

John Steinbeck, The Red Pony

2. The truck drivers, **when they heard that Maxie Hammerman had been released**, were furious.

Jean Merrill, The Pushcart War

3. The thunder was creeping closer now, rolling angrily over the forest depths and bringing the lightning with it, ***as* we emerged from the path into the deserted Avery yard**.

Mildred D. Taylor, Roll of Thunder, Hear My Cry

Practice 3

Combining

Study the model, and then combine the sentences that follow into one sentence that imitates the model. Change the first sentence to resemble the first sentence part of the model, the second sentence to resemble the second sentence part of the model, etc. Compare your sentences to the ones on page 130–131 in the references. Finally, write your own sentence that imitates the model.

Example

Model: ***Before* I got two steps**, John knee-walked away from me and into the corner of the room, coughing harshly and dragging for each breath.

Stephen King, "Night Journey"

Sentences to Be Combined

a. Something happened when we almost lost hope.

b. What happened was the waiter hurried from the kitchen.

c. And the waiter hurried toward our table.

d. He was apologizing profusely.

e. And he was smiling with great sincerity.

Combination

***When* we almost lost hope**, the waiter hurried from the kitchen and toward our table, apologizing profusely and smiling with great sincerity.

Imitation

***After* we bought our tickets**, we went into the theater and toward the refreshment stand, talking excitedly and looking forward to the blockbuster movie.

1. *Model:* Strether's first question, ***when* he reached the hotel**, was about his friend.

   Henry James, The Ambassadors

   a. This is about Tabitha's favorite activity.

   b. It happened after she started up her computer.

   c. Her favorite activity was on the Internet.

2. *Model:* ***When* I was seventeen and in full obedience to my heart's urgent commands**, I stepped far from the pathway of normal life and in a moment's time ruined everything I loved.

   Scott Spencer, Endless Love

   a. This happened after the beast's heart was transformed and in complete love with Belle.

b. What happened was that he changed magically back into the handsome prince of his past.

c. And in quick time he dazzled everyone he greeted.

3. *Model:* **When she was home from her boarding-school**, I used to see her almost every day, ***because* her house was right opposite the Town Hall Annex.**

John Fowles, The Collector

a. Something happened although the Barbie doll was almost legless from so much play.

b. What happened was that Kylie used to walk her doll.

c. She would walk the doll exclusively in the morning.

d. She walked her then because her doll was just up from her night's sleep.

4. *Model:* In the week before their departure to Arrakis, ***when* all the final scurrying about had reached a nearly unbearable frenzy**, an old crone came to visit the mother of the boy, Paul.

Frank Herbert, Dune

a. This happened in the game's last seconds after the winning pass to Brennan.

b. It happened as the thunderous cheering rose to a gadzillion decibels.

c. His proud dad jumped up.

d. The reason he jumped up was to sing the fight song.

e. The fight song was of the team, the winners.

Practice 4

Expanding

At the slash mark, add an adverb clause. In Part 1, the first few words are provided and the number of words that were omitted from the original is noted after the slash mark. Approximate that number. In Part 2, add whatever seems appropriate. Compare your adverb clauses with the originals on page 131.

Part 1

1. ***Before* the girls** / [4], I heard their laughter crackling and popping like pine logs in a cooking stove.
   Maya Angelou, I Know Why the Caged Bird Sings

2. ***While* the children** / [6], their father leaned over a sofa in the adjoining room above a figure whose heart in sleep had quietly stopped its beating.
   Algernon Blackwood, "The Tradition"

3. We had gone about ten miles ***when* Harry/** [10].
   Stephen King, "Night Journey"

4. My first impression, ***as* I** / [3], was that a fire had broken out, **because the room** / [18]. (Contains two adverb clauses.)
   Sir Arthur Conan Doyle, The Hound of the Baskervilles

Part 2

5. /, the afternoon wind struck him and blew up his hair and ruffled his shirt.
   John Steinbeck, The Red Pony

6. They were hateful sharks, bad smelling, scavengers as well as killers, and /, they would bite at an oar or the rudder of a boat.
   Ernest Hemingway, The Old Man and the Sea

7. A child with a crooked mouth and twisted hands can very quickly and easily develop a set of very crooked and twisted attitudes both towards himself and life in general, especially /.
   Christy Brown, My Left Foot

8. /, and /, she decided that in spite of the instructions on the radio, she simply could not face starting out all over again.
   John Hersey, Hiroshima

Putting the Adverb Clause to Work

The sentences below, all opening sentences of famous novels, contain adverb clauses beginning with *when.* The authors recognize the importance of a good beginning for their stories, so they took great care in writing those opening sentences.

Study the sentences and then write an effective sentence similar to the ones in the list. Pretend that you are starting your own novel. Option: Finish your novel after your great start!

First Sentences of Famous Novels

1. ***When* a journey begins badly**, it rarely ends well.
   Jules Verne, The Floating Island

2. ***When* Harold was three for four**, his father and mother took him to a swimming pool.
   John Updike, Trust Me

3. ***When* Danny came home from the army**, he learned that he was an heir and an owner of property.
   John Steinbeck, Tortilla Flat

4. ***When* he was nearly thirteen**, my brother Jem got his arm badly broken at the elbow.
   Harper Lee, To Kill a Mockingbird

5. ***When* I left my office that beautiful spring day**, I had no idea what was in store for me.
   Wilson Rawls, Where the Red Fern Grows

6. ***When* I crossed the Ashley River my senior year in my gray 1959 Chevrolet**, I was returning with confidence and even joy.
   Pat Conroy, The Lords of Discipline

7. ***When* Gregor Samsa woke up one morning from unsettling dreams**, he found himself changed in his bed into a monstrous vermin.
   Franz Kafka, The Metamorphosis

8. ***When* Augustus came out on the porch**, the blue pigs were eating a rattlesnake—not a very big one.
   Larry McMurtry, Lonesome Dove

9. ***When* a day that you happen to know is Wednesday starts off by sounding like Sunday**, there is something seriously wrong somewhere.
   John Wyndham, The Day of the Triffids

10. ***When* I think back now**, I realize that the only thing John Wilson and I actually ever had in common was the fact that at one time or another each of us ran over someone with an automobile.

               Paul Viertel, White Hunter, Black Heart

11. ***When* you are getting on in years (but not ill, of course)**, you get very sleepy at times, and the hours seem to pass like lazy cattle moving across a landscape.

               James Hilton, Goodbye, Mr. Chips

12. ***When* Mr. Bilbo Baggins of Bag End announced that he would shortly be celebrating his eleventy-first birthday with a party of special magnificence**, there was much talk and excitement in Hobbiton.

               J. R. R. Tolkien, The Fellowship of the Ring

13. ***When* he finished packing**, he walked out onto the third-floor porch of the barracks, brushing the dust from his hands, a very neat and deceptively slim young man in the summer khakis that were still early morning fresh.

               James Jones, From Here to Eternity

14. She only stopped screaming ***when* she died**.

               Jeffrey Archer, Kane and Abel

15. I get the willies ***when* I see closed doors**.

               Joseph Heller, Something Happened

16. Brenda was six ***when* she fell out of the apple tree**.

               Norman Mailer, The Executioner's Song

17. It happened that green and crazy summer ***when* Frankie was twelve years old**.

               Carson McCullers, The Member of the Wedding

18. It was four o'clock ***when* the ceremony was over and the carriages began to arrive**.

               Upton Sinclair, The Jungle

19. Many years later, as he faced the firing squad, Colonel Aureliano Buendia was to remember that distant afternoon ***when* his father took him to discover ice**.

               Gabriel Garcia Marquez, One Hundred Years of Solitude

20. I was leaning against a bar in a speakeasy of Fifty-second Street, waiting for Nora to finish her Christmas shopping, **when a girl got up from the table where she had been sitting with three other people and came over to me**.

Dashiell Hammett, The Thin Man

Reviewing the Tools

Earlier in this worktext you learned to identify and use seven skills habitually used by professional writers. Here you will refresh your understanding of those skills to prepare you to use them as tools in your own writing to build better sentences.

Practice 1

Each sentence has one or more of the skills taught earlier. Using the abbreviations that follow, identify the underlined skills. Check your answers in the references on page 132. *Note:* If you need to review the skill, the page numbers are in parentheses.

Review These Pages

Phrases

AP	=	appositive phrase	*(pages 2–11)*
AB	=	absolute phrase	*(pages 24–33)*
P	=	present participial phrase	*(pages 12–23)*
PP	=	past participial phrase	*(pages 12–23)*
PREP	=	prepositional phrase	*(pages 34–43)*

Clauses

ADJC	=	adjective clause	*(pages 44–53)*
ADVC	=	adverb clause	*(pages 54–65)*

1. The writer, (a) <u>an old man with a white mustache</u>, had some difficulty in getting into bed.
   Sherwood Anderson, Winesburg, Ohio

2. She saw smooth metal paneling, (a) <u>with no hand grips</u>.
   Michael Crichton, The Lost World

3. (a) <u>One of eleven brothers and sisters</u>, Harriet was a moody, willful child.
   Langston Hughes, "Road to Freedom"

4. The man looked up, (a) <u>his dark, grizzled features full of horror</u>, and nodded blankly.

Caleb Carr, The Alienist

5. His fists, (a) <u>huge brown rocks at the ends of those arms,</u> were closed.

Stephen King, "The Bad Death of Eduard Delacroix"

6. Mr. Sherlock Holmes, (a) <u>who was usually very late in the mornings except upon those not infrequent occasions when he was up all night</u>, was seated (b) <u>at the breakfast table</u>.

Sir Arthur Conan Doyle, The Hound of the Baskervilles

7. (a) <u>His head aching</u>, (b) <u>his throat sore</u>, he forgot to light the cigarette.

Sinclair Lewis, Cass Timberlane

8. (a) <u>Crouched on the edge of the plateau</u>, the schoolmaster looked (b) <u>at the deserted expanse</u>.

Albert Camus, <u>Exile and the Kingdom</u>

9. Now, (a) <u>facing the bull</u>, he was conscious of many things (b) <u>at the same time</u>.

Ernest Hemingway, "The Undefeated"

10. (a) <u>When I told the kids we were going to work in groups</u>, they cheered and clapped, (b) <u>except for Attiba</u>.

LouAnne Johnson, My Posse Don't Do Homework

11. (a) <u>Crumpled there</u>, he held his temples desperately (b) <u>with both hands</u> and was wretchedly sick.

Bill and Vera Cleaver, Where the Lilies Bloom

12. (a) <u>About the bones</u>, ants were ebbing away, (b) <u>their pincers full of meat</u>.

Doris Lessing, African Stories

13. A little house, (a) <u>perched on high piles</u>, appeared black (b) <u>in the distance</u>.

Joseph Conrad, "The Lagoon"

14. (a) <u>While I was shaving</u>, Judith came in and kissed me, then went (b) <u>to the kitchen</u> to make breakfast.

Michael Crichton, A Case of Need

15. Taran, (a) <u>hunched against a tree root</u>, pulled his cloak closer (b) <u>about his shoulders</u>.
    Lloyd Alexander, The Book of Three

16. The West Side streets (a) <u>of Manhattan</u> were our private playground, (b) <u>a cement kingdom where we felt ourselves to be nothing less than absolute rulers</u>.
    Lorenzo Carcaterra, Sleepers

17. (a) <u>When she was home from her boarding-school</u>, I used to see her almost every day sometimes, (b) <u>because their house was right opposite the Town Hall Annex</u>.
    John Fowles, The Collector

18. (a) <u>On the way</u> (b) <u>to the island</u>, Ledare had told me sweetly that it was time we began seeing other people, that her parents were insisting that we break up soon (c) <u>after graduation</u>.
    Pat Conroy, Beach Music

19. I went over and took a teakwood chair (a) <u>with cushions</u> (b) <u>of emerald-green silk</u>, (c) <u>sitting stiffly with my brief case across my knees</u>.
    Ralph Ellison, Invisible Man

20. The boys, (a) <u>as they talked to the girls from Marcia Blaine School</u>, stood on the far side of their bicycles holding the handlebars, (b) <u>which established a protective fence of bicycle between the sexes</u>, and the impression that (c) <u>at any moment</u> the boys were likely to be away.
    Muriel Spark, The Prime of Miss Jean Brodie

21. Buck stood and looked on, (a) <u>the successful champion</u>, (b) <u>the dominant primordial beast</u>, (c) <u>who had made his kill and found it good</u>.
    Jack London, The Call of the Wild

22. (a) <u>With a squall</u> (b) <u>of pain and rage</u>, the big cat rolled over (c) <u>on his side</u>, (d) <u>dragging Little Ann with him</u>.
    Wilson Rawls, Where the Red Fern Grows

23. All day the heat had been barely supportable, but (a) <u>at evening</u> a breeze arose (b) <u>in the West</u>, (c) <u>blowing from</u>

the heart of the setting sun and from the ocean, (d) which lay unseen and unheard behind the scrubby foothills.
Evelyn Waugh, The Loved One

24. (a) For Clarentine Flett, (b) lying in a coma after being knocked down by a bicycle at the corner of Portage and Main, religion is a soft flurry of petals, (c) drifting and (d) settling peacefully on the evening of her life.
Carol Shields, The Stone Diaries

25. (a) To their left, (b) beyond a strip of grass, was the front (c) of a large high building (d) in grey stone.
Kingsley Amis, The Anti-Death League

26. His favorite mail (a) from a famous person, (b) because it took him back to a happier time during his childhood, was the note Walt Disney had sent him back (c) in 1935, (d) when, at the age of thirteen, he had submitted some funny-animal drawings and gag ideas on the chance that he could go to work for the Disney studio, (e) making then a new kind of animated, feature-length film called *Snow White and the Seven Dwarfs*.
Oscar Hijuelos, Mr. Ives' Christmas

27. I was (a) on the upper rail (b) of our small corral, (c) soaking in the late afternoon sun, (d) when I saw him far down the road where it swung into the valley from the open plain beyond.
Jack Schaefer, Shane

28. He threw himself (a) at the door (b) of his cell and thrust his arms out (c) between the bars, (d) reaching as far as he could, (e) crying the mouse's name over and over.
Stephen King, "The Bad Death of Eduard Delacroix"

29. (a) From the small crossed window (b) of his room (c) above the stable (d) in the brickyard, Yakov Bok saw people (e) in their long overcoats running somewhere early that morning, (f) everybody in the same direction.
Bernard Malamud, The Fixer

30. (a) Tugged here and there in his stockinged feet, (b) bewildered by the numbers, (c) staggered by so much raw

flesh, Dr. Sasaki lost all sense (d) <u>of profession</u> and stopped working (e) <u>as a skillful surgeon and a sympathetic man</u>, and became an automaton, (f) <u>mechanically wiping</u>, (g) <u>daubing</u>, (h) <u>winding</u>, (i) <u>wiping</u>, (j) <u>daubing</u>, (k) <u>winding</u>.

John Hersey, Hiroshima

*P*ractice 2

Imitate six of the model sentences from Practice 1, one from each group. Then exchange your imitations with a partner, and both partners should guess what models were used for each other's imitations.

Group 1: Models 1–5

Group 2: Models 6–10

Group 3: Models 11–15

Group 4: Models 16–20

Group 5: Models 21–25

Group 6: Models 26–30

2

Positions for Sentence Variety

Here you will learn how professional writers construct different parts of their sentences—opening, subject-verb split, and closing—using the tools that you learned in Part 1 to fill those positions.

Skill 7

Sentence Opener Position

Identifying the Sentence Opener Position

Here's a list of sentences, all written by professional writers, but with some parts deleted.

1. The outlook was anything but bright.

2. No more than six or seven were out on the cold, open platform.

3. He started along the main corridor on his way toward the stairs.

4. Elizabeth Willard lighted a lamp and put it on a dressing table that stood by the door.

5. Manuel noticed the points of the bull's horns.

Now compare those sentences with the originals that follow. Notice that it's the **boldface** parts (sentence openers) that account for the professional sentence variety.

1a. **With the newcomers hopeless and forlorn, and the old team worn out by twenty-five hundred miles of continuous trail**, the outlook was anything but bright.

Jack London, The Call of the Wild

2a. **Of the twenty-some young men who were waiting at the station for their dates to arrive on the ten-fifty-two**, no more than six or seven were out on the cold, open platform.

J. D. Salinger, Franny and Zooey

3a. **With the blood specimen in his left hand, walking in a kind of distraction that he had felt all morning,**

probably because of the dream and his restless night, he started along the main corridor on his way toward the stairs.

> *John Hersey,* Hiroshima

4a. **In her room, tucked away in a corner of the old Willard House**, Elizabeth Willard lighted a lamp and put it on a dressing table that stood by the door.

> *Sherwood Anderson,* Winesburg, Ohio

5a. **Standing still now and spreading the red cloth of the muleta with the sword, pricking the point into the cloth so that the sword, now held in his left hand, spread the red flannel like the jib of a boat**, Manuel noticed the points of the bull's horns.

> *Ernest Hemingway, "The Undefeated"*

Characteristics of a Sentence Opener

A sentence opener is any word, phrase, or clause—or mixture of words, phrases, or clauses—at the beginning of a sentence.

Words as Sentence Openers

Adjective

1. **Alone**, I would often speak to her.

> *Henry Miller,* Stand Still Like the Hummingbird

Adverb

2. **Eagerly**, we settled onto the muddy forest floor and waited.

> *Mildred D. Taylor,* Roll of Thunder, Hear My Cry

Phrases as Sentence Openers

Appositive

3. **A balding, smooth-faced man**, he could have been anywhere between forty and sixty.

> *Harper Lee,* To Kill a Mockingbird

Present Participle

4. **Looking over their own troops**, they saw mixed masses slowly getting into regular form.

     Stephen Crane, The Red Badge of Courage

Past Participle

5. **Amazed at the simplicity of it all**, I understood everything as never before.

     Alphonse Daudet, "The Last Lesson"

Absolute

6. **My shoulder up**, I reeled around to face Boo Radley and his bloody fangs.

     Harper Lee, To Kill a Mockingbird

Preposition

7. **In that place**, the wind prevailed.

     Glendon Swarthout, Bless the Beasts and Children

Clauses as Sentence Openers

Adverb Clause

8. **As he was walking down the street of the small town**, love hit him like a sniper's bullet.

     Oscar Hijuelos, The Fourteen Sisters of Emilio Montez O'Brien

A Mixture

Two Past Participial Phrases, Two Absolute Phrases

9. **Toweled dry and dressed, their swimsuits hanging on the line outdoors and their hair still damp**, they gathered for Devotions.

     Anne Tyler, Saint Maybe

One Present Participial Phrase, Three Absolute Phrases

10. **Standing in front of the room, her blond hair pulled back to emphasize the determination of her face, her body girdled to emphasize the determination of her**

spine, her eyes holding determinedly to anger, Miss Lass was afraid!

Rosa Guy, The Friends

One Adverb Clause, Two Present Participial Phrases

11. **As the whale made the circuit around his pool again, urging himself toward his moment of piebald beauty in the Florida sun, lifting out toward the heavy-scented odors of citrus and bougainvillea,** the audience could glimpse his white-bottomed streaking image in the water and the amazing iridescences on his black head.

Pat Conroy, The Prince of Tides

Practice 1

Unscrambling

Each scrambled sentence has sentence openers. Identify them. Then unscramble the sentence parts and write out the sentence, punctuating it correctly. Compare your sentences with the originals on page 134 in the references.

1a. to New York

b. on April 10, 1912

c. the *Titanic* left Southampton

d. on her maiden voyage

Walter Lord, A Night to Remember

2a. of paper

b. without a word

c. she took a piece

d. out of her pants pocket

Richard E. Kim, Lost Names

3a. but the most innocent pleasure

b. even then

c. our shyness prevented us from sharing anything

d. when we might have kissed and embraced unrestrainedly

Henry Miller, Stand Still Like the Hummingbird

4a.   and no one can embarrass a young person in public so much as an adult

b.   they desperately need to conform

c.   when people are young

d.   to whom he or she is related
Maya Angelou, Wouldn't Take Nothing for My Journey Now

5a.   said something about letting me go on in her place

b.   having seen me perform before Mother's friends

c.   she was very upset

d.   when she came into the wings

e.   and argued with the stage manager who
Charlie Chaplin, My Autobiography

6a.   and her children

b.   being a star in her own right

c.   she was well able

d.   earning twenty-five pounds a week

e.   to support herself
Charlie Chaplin, My Autobiography

7a.   facing the bull

b.   at the same time

c.   he was conscious

d.   now

e.   of many things
Ernest Hemingway, "The Undefeated"

8a.   but like something he had never even imagined

b.   was a figure from a dream

c.   there

d.   a strange beast that was horned and drunken-legged

e.   between two trees

f.   against a background of gaunt black rocks
Doris Lessing, "A Sunrise on the Veld"

Practice 2

Imitating

Unscramble both lists of sentence parts to make two sentences that imitate the first model. Then, imitate the same model by writing your own sentence. Finally, write imitations of the other models, making all your sentence parts like those in the model.

Model: **In the city, when the word came to him**, he walked about at night through the streets, thinking about the matter.
Sherwood Anderson, Winesburg, Ohio

Scrambled Imitations

1a.   wondering about his boss

b.   from the start

c.   Jackson worried constantly in dread during the day

d.   because the store had opened with haste

2a.   piling up the garbage

b.   when the truck arrived with junk

c.   at the dumpster

d.   they emptied it out in minutes

Other Models

1.   **At the back door, at the front door**, and **in his bedroom**, there are call buttons that, when pushed, sound a soft buzzer in the kennel behind the barn.
Dean Koontz, Intensity

2.   **At two, having eaten a lunch of fried eggs and Jerusalem artichokes**, canned pears and bread spread with clover honey, he went out to change the oil in his tractor.
David Guterson, Snow Falling on Cedars

3. **When the truck had gone, loaded with implements, with heavy tools, with beds and springs, with every movable thing that might be sold**, Tom hung around the place.
John Steinbeck, The Grapes of Wrath

Practice 3

Combining

Study the model, and then combine the sentences that follow into one sentence that imitates the model. Change the first sentence to resemble the first sentence part of the model, the second sentence to resemble the second sentence part of the model, etc. Compare your sentences to the ones on page 135 in the references. Finally, write your own sentence that imitates the model.

Example

Model: **About a year later, when I had returned from the West, sadder and wiser, to return to the arms of "the widow" from whom I had run away**, we met again by chance.
Henry Miller, Stand Still Like the Hummingbird

Sentences to Be Combined

a. It occurred almost an hour ago.

b. I was mowing the lawn then.

c. I was tired and dirty.

d. The mowing of the lawn was to spruce up the appearance of the property.

e. I had heavily invested in the property.

f. The real estate agent arrived with the house-hunters.

Combination

Almost an hour ago, as I was mowing the lawn, tired and dirty, to spruce up the appearance of the property in which I had heavily invested, the real estate agent arrived with the house-hunters.

Imitation

Around the same time, when he had wrapped the manuscript, weary but satisfied, to mail it to the editor with whom he had discussed revisions, he talked twice with the advertising director.

1. *Model:* **While touring with this company,** she met and ran off with the middle-aged lord to Africa.

   Charlie Chaplin, My Autobiography

   a. This incident occurred after a meeting.

   b. The meeting was with the president.

   c. He signed the letter after meeting with the president.

   d. He delivered the letter.

   e. The person to whom he delivered it was the secretary.

2. *Model:* **When I came back in the store,** I took Momma's hand, and we both walked outside to look at the pattern.

   Maya Angelou, I Know Why the Caged Bird Sings

   a. It happened after she tried something.

   b. What she tried was the choreography.

   c. She met the director.

   d. In addition, they planned to confer with someone.

   e. The person they planned to confer with was the producer.

3. *Model:* **In all the mornings and evenings of the winter months,** young and old, big and small, were helpless victims of the bitter cold.

   Peter Abrahams, Tell Freedom

   a. It happened through all the ups of the trial.

   b. Also, it happened through all the downs of the trial.

   c. The lawyers and the judge had done something.

   d. Also, the defendant and the jury had done something.

   e. All of them had been listeners.

   f. Their listening was intense.

   g. What they listened to was the expert testimony.

4. *Model:* **Too tired to help the bush boy with fire-making, and too worn-out to eat**, he crawled wearily across his sister, put his head on her lap, and fell instantly asleep.

James V. Marshall, Walkabout

  a. Miss Simpson was too pleasant to fight.

  b. The fight would have been with the customer.

  c. The fight would have been about the return.

  d. In addition, Miss Simpson was too agreeable to resist.

  e. Miss Simpson agreed with a smile.

  f. She refunded the money without protest.

  g. Also, she remained remarkably calm.

Practice 4

Expanding

At the slash mark, add sentence openers. Compare your sentence openers with the originals on page 135.

1. /, he sat down on the edge of the couch, sat for hours without moving.

Willa Cather, "Coming, Aphrodite!"

2. /, Murphy played halfback for Yale and was named to the All-East team.

Michael Crichton, A Case of Need

3. /, the tall dark girl had been in those days much confused.

Sherwood Anderson, Winesburg, Ohio

4. /, they threaded the shimmering channel in the rowboat and, tying it to a jutting rock, began climbing the cliff together.

F. Scott Fitzgerald, Flappers and Philosophers

5. /, waves washed perilously close to the lighthouse, dashing its base with salt-tinged algae, which clung to it now like sea moss.

David Guterson, Snow Falling on Cedars

6. /, /, an invitation out meant an evening in other people's lives, and therefore freedom from his own, and it meant the possibility of laughter that would surprise him—how good it was to be alive and healthy, to have a body that had not given up in spite of everything.

Joyce Carol Oates, "The Wheel of Love"

7. /, /, she would still keep her eyes closed for a long time, then open them and relish with astonishment the blue of the brand-new curtains, replacing the apricot-pink which had filtered the morning light into the room where she had slept as a girl.

Colette, "The Hand"

8. /, /, Ariel was eighteen years old, no longer a girl but a lovely young woman.

Dean Koontz, Intensity

Putting the Sentence Opener Position to Work

To practice using sentence openers, add one to each of the sentences in the paragraphs that follow. Each paragraph should describe *five minutes* in the life of someone on the job. Use a variety of types of openers. *Important:* Save your paragraphs to use again on pages 93 and 104.

Example
Five Minutes in the Life of a Boxer

Without Openers

Jack entered the ring. His opponent was already waiting there. Jack listened to the referee. Jack took off his robe and waited for the bell.

With Openers

Lifting the rope and heading for his corner, Jack entered the ring. **Sparring to warm up, punching the air with a rapid pistonlike movement**, his opponent was already waiting there. **Worried more than usual because his opponent would be his toughest yet**, Jack listened to the referee. **His trainer at his side whispering encouragement, his body tensing for the opening round, ready to fight and give it his best**, Jack took off his robe and waited for the bell.

---

1. Five Minutes in the Life of a Plumber
   The plumber rang the doorbell. Mr. Cranston came to the door. The plumber listened calmly to his complaints and then went to the washing machine in the basement. The plumber went to work.

2. Five Minutes in the Life of a Supermarket Cashier
   The checkout cashier picked up the first item in the load of groceries. She struck up a conversation with the customer. She tried not to think about the three hours left before quitting time. She packed the customer's bag carefully.

3. Five Minutes in the Life of—[You Decide!]
   Write a four-sentence paragraph, using a detailed, varied sentence opener in each of the sentences.

Skill 8

Subject-Verb Split Position

Identifying the Subject-Verb Split Position

Here's a list of sentences, all written by well-known writers, but with some parts deleted. The subject and the verb are indicated.

1. Her hair made an ash-blond crown.
   ^S   ^V
2. The all-powerful auto industry was suddenly forced to *listen* for a change.
3. Their restless activity had given him his name.
4. Henry Strader made the same joke every morning.
5. The coming of industrialism has worked a tremendous change in the lives and in the habits of thought of our people of Mid-America.

Now compare those sentences above with the originals that follow. Notice that it's the **boldface** parts (Subject-Verb splits) that account for the professional sentence variety.

1a. Her hair, **braided and wrapped around her head**, made an ash-blond crown.

John Steinbeck, The Grapes of Wrath

2a. The all-powerful auto industry, **accustomed to telling the customer what sort of car he wanted**, was suddenly forced to *listen* for a change.

Jessica Mitford, The American Way of Death

3a. Their restless activity, **like unto the beating of the wings of an imprisoned bird**, had given him his name.

Sherwood Anderson, Winesburg, Ohio

4a. Henry Strader, **an old man who had been on the farm since Jesse came into possession and who before**

> **David's time had never been known to make a joke**, made the same joke every morning.
> *Sherwood Anderson,* Winesburg, Ohio

5a. The coming of industrialism, **attended by all the roar and rattle of affairs, the shrill cries of millions of new voices that have come among us from overseas, the going and coming of trains, the growth of cities, the building of the inter-urban car lines that weave in and out of towns and past farm-houses, and now in these days the coming of automobiles**, has worked a tremendous change in the lives and in the habits of thought of our people of Mid-America.
> *Sherwood Anderson,* Winesburg, Ohio

Characteristics of a Subject-Verb Split

A subject-verb split is any word, phrase, or clause—or mixture of words, phrases, or clauses—between a subject and verb.

Words as Subject-Verb Splits

Adjective

1. A sigh, **short** and **faint**, marked an almost imperceptible pause, and then his words flowed on, without a stir, without a gesture.
   > *Joseph Conrad, "The Lagoon"*

Adverb

2. He, **suddenly**, soared up out of the water in a fountain of spray, turning as he fell.
   > *Willard Price,* The Killer Shark

Phrases as Subject-Verb Splits

Appositive

3. Poppa, **a good quiet man**, spent the last hours before our parting moving aimlessly about the yard, keeping to himself and avoiding me.
   > *Gordon Parks, "My Mother's Dream for Me"*

Present Participle

4. Pedro, **sitting in his hammock**, was eating a slice of watermelon and thinking of Tita.

    Laura Esquivel, Like Water for Chocolate

Past Participle

5. Ethan, **alerted now for signs of the wonderful in his daughter**, was struck by the strange fact the she was making conversation.

    John Updike, "Man and Daughter in the Cold"

Absolute

6. High in the air, a little figure, **his hands thrust in his short jacket pockets**, stood staring out to the sea.

    Katherine Mansfield, "The Voyage"

Preposition

7. Bearded men, **in sad-colored garments, and gray, steeple-crowned hats**, intermixed with women.

    Nathaniel Hawthorne, The Scarlet Letter

Clauses as Subject-Verb Splits:

Adjective Clause

8. Chips, **who was in charge**, stood a little way off, talking to a man at the gate of a cottage.

    James Hilton, Goodbye, Mr. Chips

Adverb Clause

9. Raisl, **before they were married**, had made the bag out of a piece of her dress and embroidered it with the tablets of the Ten Commandments.

    Bernard Malamud, The Fixer

A Mixture

Appositive Phrase, Present Participial Phrase, Prepositional Phrase

10. The clerk, **a snappy-looking fellow, wearing a red bow tie, with a pink baby face but not a wisp of**

hair on his head, tried to talk me into buying one big bottle.

Robert Cormier, Take Me Where the Good Times Are

Appositive Phrase, Absolute Phrase

11. The market, **a large open square with wooden houses on two sides, some containing first-floor shops,** was crowded with peasant carts laden with grains, vegetables, wood, hides, and whatnot.

Bernard Malamud, The Fixer

Practice 1

Unscrambling

Each scrambled sentence has subject-verb splits. Identify them. Then unscramble the sentence parts and write out the sentence, punctuating it correctly. Compare your sentences with the originals on page 136 in the references.

1a.   in getting into bed

  b.   the writer

  c.   had some difficulty

  d.   an old man with a white mustache

Sherwood Anderson, Winesburg, Ohio

2a.   suddenly arose and advanced toward him

  b.   absorbed in his own idea

  c.   his terror grew until his whole body shook

  d.   when Jesse Bentley

Sherwood Anderson, Winesburg, Ohio

3a.   the twins

  b.   in a detached way

  c.   smeary in the face, eating steadily from untidy paper sacks of sweets

  d.   followed them

Katherine Anne Porter, Ship of Fools

4a.   the sinuous, limbless body

  b.   his hands

    c.   ran up and down the soft-skinned baby body

    d.   beyond control

                               Judith Merrill, "That Only a Mother"

5a.   and edged into the witness box

    b.   Horace Whaley

    c.   swore softly on the courtroom Bible

    d.   the Island Coroner

                         David Guterson, Snow Falling on Cedar

6a.   felt more pleasure than pain

    b.   fresh from the pounding of Johnnie's fists

    c.   his face

    d.   and the driving snow

    e.   in the wind

                       Stephen Crane, "The Blue Hotel"

7a.   with the knotted, cracked joints and the square, horn-thick nails

    b.   the big hands

    c.   of a shed after work

    d.   hang loose off the wrist bone

    e.   hung on the wall

    f.   like clumsy, homemade tools

                       Robert Penn Warren,
          "The Patented Gate and the Mean Hamburger"

8a.   who had brought flowers and baskets of fruit

    b.   took leisurely leave

    c.   their thin dark hair sleeked down over their ears, their thin-soled black slippers too short in the toes and badly run over at high heels

    d.   of a half dozen local young men

e.   the four pretty, slatternly Spanish girls

f.   with kisses all around

Katherine Anne Porter, Ship of Fools

Practice 2

Imitating

Unscramble both lists of sentence parts to make two sentences that imitate the first model. Then, imitate the same model by writing your own sentence. Finally, write imitations of the other models, making all of your sentence parts like those in the model. *Note:* The model contains two subject-verb splits, one in each clause.

> *Model:* In the presence of George Willard, Wing Biddlebaum, who **for twenty years had been the town mystery**, lost something of his timidity, and his shadowy personality, **submerged in a sea of doubts**, came forth to look at the world.
>
> *Sherwood Anderson,* Winesburg, Ohio

Scrambled Imitations

1a.   warned the traffic to make way

  b.   in the flurry of traffic

  c.   who only an hour ago had been asleep

  d.   wailing like a giant in agony

  e.   the ambulance driver

  f.   and his siren

  g.   gripped the steering wheel

2a.   derived from his year's self-control with alcohol

  b.   near the field of wheat

  c.   who a year ago had been an irresponsible drunk

  d.   tough-skinned Jasper

  e.   allowed him to concentrate on farming

f.   and his serenity

g.   walked peacefully among his crops

Other Models

1. Dozens of family photos, **framed in dull brass or varnished wood**, stood on an ivory lace runner.

    Anne Tyler, Saint Maybe

2. The gwythaints, **which at a distance had seemed no more than dry leaves in the wind**, grew larger and larger, as they plunged toward horse and riders.

    Lloyd Alexander, The Book of Three

3. Ricky, **nineteen, not overburdened with brains**, worked down at Sonny's Sunoco.

    Stephen King, Needful Things

Practice 3

Combining
Study the model, and then combine the sentences that follow into one sentence that imitates the model. Change the first sentence to resemble the first sentence part of the model, the second sentence to resemble the second sentence part of the model, etc. Compare your sentences to the ones on page 137 in the references. Finally, write your own sentence that imitates the model.

Example

Model: At daybreak Rainsford, **lying near the swamp**, was awakened by a sound that made him know that he had new things to learn about fear.

    Richard Connell, "The Most Dangerous Game"

Sentences to Be Combined

a. It occurred before the game.

b. Winston was the one to whom it happened.

c. He was suffering from nervousness.

d. Winston was telephoned.

e. A fellow player called him.

f. The player told him something.

g. What he told Winston was that Winston had several plays.

h. The plays Winston had to revise.

i. The revision had to take place before the game.

Combination

Before the game Winston, **suffering from nervousness**, was telephoned by a fellow player who told him that Winston had several plays to revise before the game.

Imitation

Near the junkyard Mr. Pauley, **jogging through the intersection**, was surprised by a truck, that made him realize that he should schedule his route to arrive after dawn.

---

1. *Model:* **Van'ka Zhukov,** a boy of nine who had been apprenticed to the shoemaker Alyakhin three months ago, was staying up that Christmas eve.

   Anton Chekhov, "Van'ka"

   a. Nielsen Rating Service was in operation.

   b. This service is a determiner of TV ratings.

   c. The ratings were those that had been accepted by the TV networks that season.

   d. The operation the service was engaged in was surveying this morning.

2. *Model:* **Dvoira,** the dark-uddered cow, was out in the field behind the hut, browsing under a leafless poplar tree, and Yakov went out to her.

   Bernard Malamud, The Fixer

   a. The cook was concerned about something.

   b. He was a fine-bellied gourmet.

   c. He was back in the kitchen at the closet freezer.

d. There, he was ruminating about the latest beef selections.

e. But, the butcher reassured him.

3. *Model:* When his father, **who was old and twisted with toil**, made over to him the ownership of the farm and seemed content to creep away to a corner and wait for death, he shrugged his shoulders and dismissed the old man from his mind.

Sherwood Anderson, Winesburg, Ohio

a. The thunderstorm was the cause of something.

b. It had been sudden and fierce in downpour.

c. It brought to the fields the rain for the crops.

d. In addition, it was steady enough to remain in the parched land and penetrate to the roots.

e. The result was that the plants raised their branches.

f. Another result was that they arched their stems toward the sun.

4. *Model:* Warren McIntyre, **who casually attended Yale, being one of the unfortunate stags**, felt in his dinner-coat pocket for a cigarette and strolled out onto the wide, semi-dark veranda, where couples were scattered at tables, filling the lantern-hung night with vague words and hazy laughter.

F. Scott Fitzgerald, "Bernice Bobs Her Hair"

a. This is about Janice Larson.

b. She successfully finished auto-mechanics.

c. She had been one of few girls in the course.

d. She tried with great persistence for a related job.

e. In addition, she applied to several employment agencies.

f. At those agencies, counselors were surprised at her sex.

g. They described her prospects.

h. The description of her prospects was done with guarded optimism but sincere hope.

Practice 4

Expanding
At the slash mark, add subject-verb splits. Compare your subject-verb splits with the originals on page 138.

1. When the match went out, the old man, /, peeped into the little window.

   Anton Chekhov, "The Bet"

2. The country house, /, was most enjoyable.

   James Thurber, "Mr. Monroe Holds the Fort"

3. At once Buntaro slid an arrow from the quiver and, /, set up the bow, raised it, drew back the bowstring to eye level and released the shaft with savage, almost poetic liquidity.

   James Clavell, Shogun

4. These three trains, /, confirmed my fears that traffic was not maintained by night on this part of the line.

   Winston Churchill, "I Escape from the Boers"

5. The first opportune minute came that very afternoon, and Cress, /, went in tears to her room.

   Jessamyn West, "Cress Delahanty"

6. And my departure, which, /, stank of betrayal, was my only means of proving, or redeeming, that love, my only hope.

   James Baldwin, "Every Good-bye Ain't Gone"

7. Only a frying pan, /, remained.

   Naomi Hintze, "The Lost Gold of Superstitions"

8. His little dark eyes, /, and his mouth, /, made him look attentive and studious. (Contains two subject-verb splits.)

   Albert Camus, Exile and the Kingdom

Putting the Subject-Verb Split Position to Work
To practice using subject-verb splits, add one to each of the sentences in the paragraphs that follow. Each paragraph should describe *five minutes* in the life of someone on the job. Use a variety of types of subject-verb splits. *Note:* Use the paragraphs you have already written from "Putting the Sentence Opener

Position to Work" on page 81. *Important:* Save your paragraphs to use again on page 104.

Example
Five Minutes in the Life of a Boxer

Without Openers or Splits

Jack entered the ring. His opponent was already waiting there. Jack looked at the referee. Jack took off his robe and waited for the bell.

With Openers

Lifting the rope and heading for his corner, Jack entered the ring. **Sparring to warm up, punching the air with a rapid pistonlike movement**, his opponent was already waiting there. **Worried more than usual because his opponent would be his toughest yet**, Jack llistened to the referee. **His trainer at his side whispering encouragement, his body tensing for the opening round, ready to fight and give it his best**, Jack took off his robe and waited for the bell.

With Openers and New Splits (Underlined)

Lifting the rope and heading for his corner, Jack, <u>who was the contender in tonight's event</u>, entered the ring. **Sparring to warm up, punching the air with a rapid pistonlike movement**, his opponent, <u>the reigning champion, the guy everyone had put money on</u>, was already waiting there. **Worried more than usual because his opponent would be his toughest yet**, Jack, <u>the lights glaring in their domes above, the crowd blaring throughout the arena</u>, listened to the referee. **His trainer at his side whispering encouragement, his body tensing for the opening round, ready to fight and give it his best**, Jack, <u>saying a silent prayer to the patron saint of hopeless causes</u>, took off his robe and waited for the bell.

---

1. Five Minutes in the Life of a Plumber
   The plumber rang the doorbell. Mr. Cranston came to the door. The plumber listened calmly to his complaints and then went to the washing machine in the basement. The plumber went to work.

2. Five Minutes in the Life of a Supermarket Cashier
   The checkout cashier picked up the first item in the load of groceries. She struck up a conversation with the customer.

She tried not to think about the three hours left before quitting time. She packed the customer's bag carefully.

3. Five Minutes in the Life of—[You Decide!]
   Write a four-sentence paragraph, using a detailed, varied subject-verb split in each of the sentences.

*S*kill 9

Sentence Closer Position

*I*dentifying the Sentence Closer Position

Here's a list of sentences, all written by professional writers, but with some parts deleted.

1. It ran.
2. He strode forward.
3. He hung around L.A.
4. By and by, one group after another came straggling back to the mouth of the cave.
5. I would huddle.

Now compare those sentences above with the originals. Notice that it's the **boldface** parts (sentence closers) that account for the professional sentence variety.

1a.   It ran, **its pelvic bones crushing aside trees and bushes, its taloned feet clawing damp earth, leaving prints six inches deep wherever it settled its weight**.
Ray Bradbury, "A Sound of Thunder"

2a.   He strode forward, **crushing ants with each step, and brushing them off his clothes, till he stood above the skeleton, which lay sprawled under a small bush**.
Doris Lessing, "A Sunrise on the Veld" from African Stories

3a.   He hung around L.A., **broke most of the time, working as an usher in movie theatres, getting an occasional part as an extra on the lots, or a bit on TV, dreaming and yearning and hungry, eating cold spaghetti out of the can**.
John Dos Passos, "The Sinister Adolescents"

4a.   By and by, one group after another came straggling back to
      the mouth of the cave, **panting, hilarious, smeared from
      head to foot with tallow drippings, daubed with clay,
      and entirely delighted with the success of the day.**
                    Mark Twain, The Adventures of Tom Sawyer

5a.   I would huddle, **listening to their noise in the darkness,
      my eyebrows lifted, my lips pursed, the hair on the
      back of my neck standing up like pigs' bristle.**
                                  John Gardner, Grendel

Characteristics of a Sentence Closer

A sentence closer is any word, phrase, or clause—or mixture of
words, phrases, or clauses—at the end of a sentence.

Words as Sentence Closers

Adjective

1. Blue Elk went out, **hurt** and **angry**.
                            Hal Borland, When the Legends Die

Adverb

2. Neither boy had on shoes, and their Sunday clothing,
   patched and worn, hung upon their frail frames, **loosely**.
                    Mildred D. Taylor, Roll of Thunder, Hear My Cry

Phrases as Sentence Closers

Appositive

3. He remembered a chipmunk he had as a small boy, **a pet
   that came when he called and sat in his hand**.
                            Hal Borland, When the Legends Die

Present Participle

4.   I began to walk about the room, **examining various
     indefinite objects in the half darkness**.
                              F. Scott Fitzgerald, The Great Gatsby

Past Participle

5. Then the doctor hurried in, **followed by his man**.

John Steinbeck, The Pearl

Absolute

6. Eugie came clomping down the stairs and into the kitchen, **his head drooping with sleepiness**.

Gina Berriault, "The Stone Boy"

Preposition

7. The sea is high again today, **with a thrilling flush of wind**.

Lawrence Durrell, Justine

Clauses as Sentence Closers

Adjective Clause

8. Hatsuyo Nakamura, weak and destitute, began a courageous struggle to keep her children and herself alive, **which would last for many years**.

John Hersey, Hiroshima

Adverb Clause

9. He began to dig again, driving his spade deep into the rich, black garden soil **while the robin hopped about very busily employed**.

Frances Hodgson Burnett, The Secret Garden

A Mixture

Two Present Participial Phrases, One Appositive Phrase, One Adjective Clause

10. He stayed there, **puttering in his garden, talking to his beans and chilies and even to himself, an old man with a hump on his broken back, who once was a rodeo rider**.

Hal Borland, When the Legends Die

One Past Participial Phrase, One Present Participial Phrase, Two Past Participial Phrases, Three Present Participial Phrases

11. The guests continued to come, **dressed for high summer** and **hoping for swimming weather, convinced that**

Provence enjoyed a Mediterranean climate and **dismayed to find us in sweaters, lighting fires in the evening, drinking winter wines**, and **eating winter food**.

Peter Mayle, A Year in Provence

Practice 1

Unscrambling

Each scrambled sentence has sentence closers. Identify them, and then unscramble the sentence parts to make a good sentence. Add commas where needed. Write the completed sentence. Finally, compare yours with the original sentences on page 138–139 in the references.

1a. limping

 b. he went on

William Faulkner, "Dry September"

2a. for what reason neither grand-parent would tell

 b. from Grandpa

 c. she was separated

Charlie Chaplin, My Autobiography

3a. not rolling

 b. it was a heavy sound

 c. hard and sharp

Theodore Taylor, "The Cay"

4a. trying to be together as long as possible

 b. and so we sent to the station, across the meadow

 c. taking the longer way

Gerda Weissmann Klein, All But My Life

5a. and even changing the well-known scents

 b. filling the whole room

 c. sometimes a gaggle of them came to the store

 d. chasing out the air

Maya Angelou, I Know Why the Caged Bird Sings

6a. a shadow

  b. hour after hour

  c. motionless

  d. he stood there silent

  e. carved in ebony and moonlight
                                        James V. Marshall, Walkabout

7a. a gigantic race

  b. before the creation

  c. Prometheus was one of the Titans

  d. who inhabited the earth

  e. of man
                          Thomas Bulfinch, "Prometheus and Pandora"

8a. light flickered on bits of ruby glass

  b. and on sensitive capillary hairs

  c. in the nylon-brushed nostrils

  d. on rubber-padded paws

  e. its eight legs spidered under it

  f. of the creature that quivered gently, gently
                                        Ray Bradbury, Fahrenheit 451

Practice 2

Imitating
Unscramble both lists of sentence parts to make two sentences
that imitate the first model. Then, imitate the same model by
writing your own sentence. Finally, write imitations of the other
models, making all of your sentence parts like those in the
model.

  Model: I would huddle, **listening to their noise in the
darkness, my eyebrows lifted, my lips pursed, the hair on
the back of my neck standing up like pigs' bristle**.
                                        John Gardner, Grendel

Scrambled Imitations

1a.   deciding about their agenda for the sales meeting

b.   they would meet

c.   their opinions uncertain

d.   the leader of the group of section chiefs shouting out like a huckster

e.   their interest high

2a.   their stems poised

b.   she smiled

c.   the arrangement of the bouquet of roses looking like a prize-winner

d.   their blossoms in full bloom

e.   glancing at the flowers in the vase

Other Models

1.   Many of the picnickers had eaten to excess and now sat heavy and dulled in the sun, **which poured over the scene a clear, clean radiance, a piercing island summer light**.
       David Guterson, Snow Falling on Cedars

2.   She wears silver earrings in the shape of starfish, **an eccentric touch, the last vestige of her days of piracy**.
       Margaret Atwood, "The Bog Man"

3.   He sat quite still on a bench in a constantly moving, muttering, moaning, outraged population of maniacs, **some in restraining jackets, others in shackles**.
       E. L. Doctorow, The Waterworks

Practice 3

Combining
Study the model, and then combine the sentences that follow into one sentence that imitates the model. Change the first

sentence to resemble the first sentence part of the model, the second sentence to resemble the second sentence part of the model, etc. Compare your sentences to the ones on page 139 in the references. Finally, write your own sentence that imitates the model.

Example

> *Model:* Before she could put a stop to it, some of their classmates scoffed at the leaf-lard-and-black-bread sandwiches they ate for lunch, **huddled in one corner of the recreation room, dressed in their boiled-out ragpickers' clothes.**
>
> *Ambrose Flack, "The Strangers That Came to Town"*

Sentences to Be Combined

a. Something happened when he selected a color for the sky.

b. One of his teachers commented on the bright hue.

c. The bright hue was the one he chose for backgrounds.

d. The bright hue was chosen with an aim.

e. The aim was toward a bold creativity.

f. The bright hue was applied.

g. The manner of application was with his most flamboyant brush strokes.

Combination

> When he selected a color for the sky, one of his teachers commented on the bright hue he chose for backgrounds, **selected with an aim toward a bold creativity, applied with his most flamboyant brush strokes.**

Imitation

> If the borrower damaged the pages of the book, several of the librarians complained about the scant concern patrons gave to proper care, **governed only by their desire for enjoyment, unconcerned about their selfish carelessness.**

1. *Model:* Close to the village there lived a lady, **a small land-owner who had an estate of about three hundred acres**.

   Leo Tolstoy, "How Much Land Does a Man Need?"

   a. This occurred high up the tree.

   b. There climbed some girls.

   c. They were little adventurers.

   d. They imagined a great escapade.

   e. The escapade was of nearly Everest proportions.

2. *Model:* Touching the ropes and knots which joined the raft together, he stooped down, **his arms and shoulders buried under the cold water, and his chin kissing the rippling surface of the river**.

   Shen T'Sung-Wen, "Under Cover of Darkness," translated by Y. Chia-Hua and Robert Payne

   a. He was inspecting the plumbing and fixtures.

   b. The plumbing and fixtures outfitted the new bathroom.

   c. He walked around.

   d. His tappings and probings were done.

   e. They were done with his expert skill.

   f. His experience was guiding his assessment.

   g. The assessment was of the work.

3. *Model:* I could see the string of camels bearing the merchandise, and the company of turbaned merchants, **carrying some of their queer old firearms, and some of their spears, journeying downward toward the plains**.

   Sir Rabindranath Tagore, "The Cabuliwallah"

   a. They could foresee a time.

   b. The time was of soldiers ending their battles.

   c. They could foresee, in addition, a period of permanent truce.

   d. They would be negotiating their disputes.

   e. The disputes were about politics.

    f. The disputes were about, in addition, many of the old arguments.

    g. They would be living peacefully within dissent.

4. *Model:* Now it is night, and I am wrapped in a traveling rug on top of a four-in-hand coach, **driving with Mother and theatrical friends, cosseted in their gaiety and laughter as our trumpeter, with clarion braggadocio, heralds us along the Kennington Road to the rhythmic jingle of harness and the beat of horses' hoofs**.

Charlie Chaplin, My Autobiography

    a. Then it was graduation.

    b. They were encouraged by a dream.

    c. The dream was of new beginnings.

    d. The new beginnings were for their lives.

    e. They were marching among friends and proud parents.

    f. They were dressed in their caps and gowns.

    g. This all happened as the orchestra stirred them.

    h. It stirred them with brass fanfares.

    i. It stirred them with its majesty of the pomp of trumpet blares.

    j. It stirred them, in addition, with the circumstances of the formal right of passage.

Practice 4

Expanding
At the slash mark, add sentence closers. Compare your sentence closers with the originals on page 140.

1. She stood out from all the other girls in the school, /.

Henry Miller, Stand Still Like the Hummingbird

2. His face was fleshy and pallid, /.

James Joyce, "The Dead"

3. The young white man who served us did it in leisurely fashion, /.

Peter Abrahams, Tell Freedom

4. His earnestness affected the boy, /.

Sherwood Anderson, Winesburg, Ohio

5. He was standing with her in the cold, /.

James Joyce, "The Dead"

6. The girl at first did not return any of the kisses, but presently she began to, and after she had put several on his cheek, she reached his lips and remained there, /.

Flannery O'Connor, "Good Country People"

7. Mary Jane gazed after her, /, /.

James Joyce, "The Dead"

8. As far down the long stretch as he could see, the trout were rising, /, /.

Ernest Hemingway, "Big Two-Hearted River: Part I"

Putting the Sentence Closer Position to Work

To practice using sentence closers, add one to each of the sentences in the paragraphs that follow. Each paragraph should describe *five minutes* in the life of someone on the job. Use a variety of types of closers. *Note:* Use the paragraphs you have already written from "Putting the Sentence Opener Position to Work" on page 81 and from "Putting the Subject-Verb Split Position to Work" on page 93.

Example
Five Minutes in the Life of a Boxer

Without Openers

Jack entered the ring. His opponent was already waiting there. Jack listened to the referee. Jack took off his robe and waited for the bell.

With Openers

Lifting the rope and heading for his corner, Jack entered the ring. **Sparring to warm up, punching the air with a rapid pistonlike movement,** his opponent was already waiting there. **Worried more than usual because his opponent would be**

his toughest yet, Jack listened to the referee. **His trainer at his side whispering encouragement, his body tensing for the opening round, ready to fight and give it his best**, Jack took off his robe and waited for the bell.

With Openers and Splits

Lifting the rope and heading for his corner, Jack, **who was the contender in tonight's event**, entered the ring. **Sparring to warm up, punching the air with a rapid pistonlike movement**, his opponent, **the reigning champion, the guy everyone had put money on**, was already waiting there. **Worried more than usual because his opponent would be his toughest yet**, Jack, **the lights glaring in their domes above, the crowd blaring throughout the arena**, listened to the referee. **His trainer at his side whispering encouragement, his body tensing for the opening round, ready to fight and give it his best**, Jack, **saying a silent prayer to the patron saint of hopeless causes**, took off his robe and waited for the bell.

With Openers, Splits, and New Closers (Underlined)

Lifting the rope and heading for his corner, Jack, **who was the contender in tonight's event**, entered the ring, <u>slowly, tentatively, as if he were stepping into a scalding bath</u>. **Sparring to warm up, punching the air with a rapid pistonlike movement**, his opponent, **the reigning champion, the guy everyone had put money on**, was already waiting there, <u>the crowd yelling out his name, a satisfied smirk on his face</u>. **Worried more than usual because his opponent would be his toughest yet**, Jack, **the lights glaring in their domes above, the crowd blaring throughout the arena**, listened to the referee, <u>a short bald guy, who spit out the rules from the corner of his mouth</u>. **His trainer at his side whispering encouragement, his body tensing for the opening round, ready to fight and give it his best**, Jack, **saying a silent prayer to the patron saint of hopeless causes**, took off his robe and waited for the bell, <u>while a drumbeat pounded inside his head</u>.

---

1. Five Minutes in the Life of a Plumber
   The plumber rang the doorbell. Mr. Cranston came to the door. The plumber listened calmly to his complaints and then went to the washing machine in the basement. The plumber went to work.

2. Five Minutes in the Life of a Supermarket Cashier
The checkout cashier picked up the first item in the load of groceries. She struck up a conversation with the customer. She tried not to think about the three hours left before quitting time. She packed the customer's bag carefully.

3. Five Minutes in the Life of—[You Decide!]
Write a four-sentence paragraph, using a detailed, varied sentence closer in each of the sentences.

*R*eviewing the Tools and Positions

*P*ractice 1

This practice reveals a secret of professional sentences: *additions*. Just as options add value to a new car, additions can add power to your sentences, making them like sentences by professional writers.

This practice provides stripped-down sentences, with the sentence parts from the original sentences, the additions, listed underneath. For each sentence—

1. Identify the sentence parts, using the abbreviations below.

2. Add the sentence parts to the stripped-down sentence, inserting them in *two positions* of the three positions (opener, subject-verb split, closer).

3. Compare your sentences with the originals on page 141 in the references.

Note: If you need to review the skill, the page numbers are in parentheses.

Review These Pages
Words

ADJ	=	**adjective**	*(pages 73, 84, 96)*
ADV	=	**adverb**	*(pages 73, 84, 96)*

Phrases

AP	=	**appositive phrase**	*(pages 2–11)*
P	=	**present participial phrase**	*(pages 12–23)*
PP	=	**past participial phrase**	*(pages 12–23)*
AB	=	**absolute phrase**	*(pages 24–33)*
PREP	=	**prepositional phrase**	*(pages 34–43)*

Clauses

ADJC = adjective clause   *(pages 44–53)*

ADVC = adverb clause   *(pages 54–65)*

1. The grass was high.
   a. around the old gravestones
   b. untended
   > *E. L. Doctorow,* The Waterworks

2. The sled went over.
   a. as they swung on the turn
   b. spilling half its load through the loose lashings
   > *Jack London,* The Call of the Wild

3. Snow White saw the faces of seven bearded, vertically challenged men.
   a. when she awoke several hours later
   b. surrounding the bed
   > *James Finn Garner,* Politically Correct Bedtime Stories

4. Fletcher Seagull conquered his sixteen-point vertical slow roll and the next day topped it off with a triple cartwheel.
   a. who loved aerobatics like no one else
   b. his feathers flashing white sunlight to a beach from which more than one furtive eye watched
   > *Richard Bach,* Jonathan Livingston Seagull

5. I fixed my attention upon Reverend Sykes.
   a. subdued
   b. who seemed to be waiting for me to settle down
   > *Harper Lee,* To Kill a Mockingbird

6. Alfred bolted across the street.
   a. wildly
   b. sidestepping a taxicab by inches
   c. ignoring the horns and curses of braking drivers
   > *Robert Lipsyte,* The Contender

7. The man was still asleep.

   a. in the far corner

   b. snoring slightly on the intaking breath

   c. his head back against the wall
   Ernest Hemingway, "The Undefeated"

8. She looked at the bright stars.

   a. at night

   b. sleeping little

   c. listening to the river
   Larry McMurtry, Streets of Laredo

9. A big kitchen table was neatly set as if for a big party.

   a. covered with one of those old-fashioned oilcloths

   b. with eight chairs

   c. two on each side of the table
   Robert Cormier, Take Me Where the Good Gimes Are

10. Caroline received uniformly high grades.

    a. an excellent student

    b. which she worked hard to get

    c. doing more than two hours of homework each day
    Lester David, Jacqueline Kennedy Onassis

11. My brothers and I buried mother.

    a. at the cemetery

    b. taking our time speaking to her

    c. as though she could hear us
    Pat Conroy, Beach Music

12. Across the open hearth sat my father.

    a. his face lit by flames

    b. leaning forward

   c. his hands outspread to his knees

   d. his shoulders tense

Christy Brown, My Left Foot

13. A structure appeared.

   a. beyond the driver

   b. beyond the windshield

   c. indistinct

   d. unidentifiable

Dean Koontz, Intensity

14. I saw Viola in her black dress.

   a. across the tops

   b. of about a hundred gravestones and many people

   c. standing on a little rise

   d. her gray hair wandering from its knot

Barbara Kingsolver, Animal Dreams

15. A young American mother sat on the edge of a steel-framed bed.

   a. in an upstairs bedroom

   b. shortly

   c. before dawn

   d. rocking her nursing daughter

Steve Estes, Called to Die

16. Wheelchair vans or ambulances or private cars parked in front of the portico and new residents were escorted in.

   a. periodically

   b. a few on their own feet

   c. others in wheelchairs

   d. some on gurneys

Tracy Kidder, Old Friends

17. Roland has stopped chopping and is sitting on the chopping block.

    a. outside the window

    b. his arms on his knees

    c. his big hands dangling

    d. staring off into the trees
    Margaret Atwood, Wilderness Tips

18. The river Rhine froze solid.

    a. On the last, cold day

    b. of December

    c. in the year 406

    d. providing the natural bridge the hundreds of thousands of hungry men, women, and children had been waiting for
    Thomas Cahill, How the Irish Saved Civilization

19. He had seemed of no more than medium height.

    a. at the university

    b. in his gray suit

    c. perhaps because he stooped so attentively to hear the slightest word from the person he was talking to

    d. perhaps because his neat, fair hair made him look somehow ineffectual
    Wallace Stegner, Crossing to Safety

20. He came up to the house again and said good-bye to the children.

    a. at three forty-five

    b. who were seated on the porch

    c. drinking apple juice and

    d. eating graham crackers and

    e. rolling pebbles back and forth
    David Guterson, Snow Falling on Cedars

21. The streets turn from the thickest dust into the direst mud.

    a. after rain, or

    b. when snowfalls thaw

    c. unnamed

    d. unshaded

    e. unpaved

Truman Capote, In Cold Blood

22. He washed his hand in the ocean and held it there for more than a minute.

    a. shifting the weight of the line to his shoulder and

    b. kneeling carefully

    c. submerged

    d. watching the blood trail away and the steady movement of the water against his hand

    e. as the boat moved

Ernest Hemingway, The Old Man and the Sea

23. Waves washed perilously close to the lighthouse.

    a. on occasions

    b. when the tide ran exceptionally high

    c. dashing its base

    d. with salt-tinged algae

    e. which clung to it now like a sea moss

David Guterson, Snow Falling on Cedars

24. He moved.

    a. turning

    b. his shoulder pressing against the wall

    c. until he was standing sideways

    d. his feet together on the narrow ledge

    e. his side hugging the wall

    f. as he faced the wide opening

        Robb White, Deathwatch

25. His right hand flew over the ledge.

    a. blindly

    b. his fingers dancing across it

    c. reaching

    d. feeling

    e. searching

    f. until his body began to drop

        Robb White, Deathwatch

26. Quoyle went to the wharf on his way to Wavey.

    a. in the morning

    b. breakfastless and

    c. shaky

    d. from seven cups

    e. of coffee

    f. heart and stomach aching

        E. Annie Proulx, The Shipping News

27. Lived a family of bears.

    a. through the thicket

    b. across the river, and

    c. in the deep, deep woods

    d. a Papa bear

    e. a Mama Bear and

    f. a Baby Bear

    g. who all lived together anthropomorphically in a little cottage as a nuclear family

        James Finn Garner, Politically Correct Bedtime Stories

28. She was sent to sleep.

    a. when Laurel was a child

    b. by the beloved reading voice

    c. under a velvety cloak

    d. of words

    d. patterned richly and

    e. stitched with gold

    f. coming straight out

    g. of a fairy tale

    h. while the voice went on reading aloud into her dreams
       Eudora Welty, The Optimist's Daughter

29. The sun began to sink.

    a. red and

    b. enormous

    c. into the western sky

    d. the moon beginning to rise

    e. on the other side

    f. of the river

    g. with its own glorious shade

    h. of red

    i. coming up out of the trees like a russet firebird
       Pat Conroy, The Prince of Tides

30. My eyes roamed.

    a. in the half-light

    b. around my room

    c. a cramped space

    d. the room of an only child

e. tidy

f. organized completely

g. with the possessory feel

h. of everything

i. in place

j. unmolested by any of the brothers and sisters I had for years longed to have and now, in my desolation, longed for with a special ache

William Styron, A Tidewater Morning

*T*he Last Practice

Add an opener, a subject-verb split, and a closer to each sentence in the paragraphs that follow. Write paragraphs that clearly prove you've accomplished the goal of this worktext: composing sentences resembling those of professional writers.

First you have to learn something, and then you can go out and do it.

Mies van der Rohe

Paragraph One: *The Detective*

(1) The detective found only one clue. (2) His partner stood over the body. (3) A crime lab professional worked around them. (4) A single bystander watched everything.

Paragraph Two: *The Doctor*

(1) The doctor prepared for surgery. (2) Her assistant was nearby. (3) The anesthesiologist stood ready. (4) The patient lay on the operating table.

Paragraph Three: *The Student*

(1) The student stared at the test. (2) The teacher stood in the front of the room. (3) The class was quiet. (4) The test was challenging.

Paragraph Four: *The Professional Writer—YOU!*

(1) [Your name] picked up a pen. (2) [He/she] thought for a minute. (3) [He/she] began to write. (4) The sentence was a dazzler!

Paragraph Five: *Your Choice*
Write your own four-sentence narrative paragraph that includes in every sentence an opener, subject-verb split, and closer.

References
Skill 1
Appositive Phrase (page 2)

Practice 1 (page 4):

1. She struggled as usual to maintain her calm, composed, friendly bearing, **a sort of mask she wore all over her body**.

2. The judge, **an old, bowlegged fellow in a pale-blue sweater**, had stopped examining the animals and was reading over some notes he had taken on the back of a dirty envelope.

3. With huge flaring nostrils, the tyrannosaur gave Baselton a smell, **a long snuffling inhalation that fluttered Baselton's trouser legs**.

4. One of them, **a slender, young man with white hands, the son of a jeweler in Winesburg**, talked continually of virginity.

5. In the late afternoon Will Henderson, **owner and editor of the *Eagle***, went over to Tom Willy's saloon.

6. The sound of the approaching grain teams was louder, **thud of big hooves on hard ground, drag of brakes**, and **the jingle of trace chains**.

7. Once Enoch Bentley, **the older one of the boys**, struck his father, **old Tom Bentley**, with the butt of a teamster's whip, and the old man seemed likely to die.

8. Mr. Mick Malloy, **tall, young secret gambler with devil-may-care eyes and a long humorous nose**, became Mr. Malloy, **tall cashier with a dignified face, a gentlemanly bank clerk, a nice sort of fellow**.

Practice 2 (page 6):

1. By the podium scholary Henrietta stood, intelligent and composed and smiling, **president and valedictorian of the senior class**.

2. Under the canopy they danced, beaming and affectionate and happy, **bride and groom in their finery**.

Practice 3 (page 7):

1. Near the statue was an obvious tourist, **an oriental lady with a Kodak camera**.

2. *Gone with the Wind*, **the movie with the most reissues**, originated as a novel of the old South by an unglamorous and unknown authoress.

3. "Missouri" is a special casserole, **a blend of potatoes and stewed tomatoes and hamburger**.

4. We were far from our destination and were making good time on the interstate, but no time to squander, and Dad wouldn't stop more than twice a day although we kids were itchy, and Mom, **a shrewd, gentle arbitrator with Solomon's mind**, circumvented some flare-ups, and those she couldn't she left to Heaven.

Practice 4 (page 9):

Part 1

1. Thus, one noontime, coming back from the office lunch downstairs a little earlier than usual, he found her and several of the foreign-family girls, as well as four of the American girls, surrounding Polish Mary, **one of the gayest and roughest of the foreign-family girls**, who was explaining in rather a high key how a certain "feller" whom she had met the night before had given her a beaded bag, and for what purpose.

2. The rest were standing around in hatless, smoky little groups of twos and threes and fours inside the heated waiting room, talking in voices that, almost without exception, sounded collegiately dogmatic, as though each young man, in his strident, conversational turn, was clearing up, once and for all, some highly controversial issue, **one that the outside, non-matriculating world had been bungling, provocatively or not, for centuries**.

3. Out in the distances the fans of windmills twinkled, turning, and about the base of each, about the drink tank, was a speckle of dark dots, **a herd of cattle grazing in moonlight and meditating upon good grass, block salt, impermanence, and love**.

4. Perhaps two or three times a year we would come together at a party, one of those teen-age affairs which last until dawn with singing and dancing and silly games such as "Kiss the Pillow," or "Post Office," **the game which permits one to call for the creature of one's choice and embrace her furtively in a dark room**.

Part 2

1. My bed was an army cot, **one of those affairs which are made wide enough to sleep on comfortably only by putting up, flat with the middle section, the two sides which ordinarily hang down like the sideboards of a drop-leaf table.**

2. He, **the enlightened man who looks afar in the dark**, had fled because of his superior perceptions and knowledge.

3. I had hardly any patience with the serious work of life which, not that it stood between me and desire, seemed to me child's play, **ugly monotonous child's play**.

4. There was Major Hunter, **a haunted little man of figures, a little man who, being a dependable unit, considered all other men either as dependable units or as unfit to live**.

Putting the Appositive Phrase to Work (page 11):
Answers will vary.

Skill 2
Participial Phrase (page 12)

Practice 1 (page 15):

1. Bernard, **wearing a black turtleneck sweater, dirty flannels, and slippers**, was waiting on the landing outside.

2. Malcolm lost his grip and fell free, **dropping helplessly down toward the far end of the trailer**.

3. **Coming down the pole**, I had a sense of being whirled violently through the air, with no control over my movements.

4. A little house, **perched on high piles**, appeared black in the distance.

5. When we had made our way downstairs, we saw the woman with the lovely complexion, Miss Pilzer, **screaming and begging to be allowed to go with her mother**.

6. He was a blind beggar, **carrying the traditional battered cane** and **thumping his way before him with the cautious, half-furtive effort of the sightless**.

7. The passengers, **emerging from the mildewed dimness of the customs sheds, blinking their eyes against the blinding sunlight**, all had the look of invalids crawling into the hospital on their last legs.

8. That winter my mother and brother came, and we set up housekeeping, **buying furniture on the installment plan, being cheated, and yet knowing no way to avoid it**.

Practice 2 (page 17):

1. As her arm whirled fast over the egg whites, her face shifted toward the cookbook and stared at it, **grimacing** and **expressing confusion and frustration over the third direction in the recipe that listed and explained more and ever more of the procedure**.

2. After Jo-Jo climbed higher onto the counter, he pulled on the doors and looked for the candy, **stretching** but **missing jars and boxes in the rear with bright colors that beckoned but hid farther and farther from his reach**.

Practice 3 (page 19):

1. A pile of new debris cluttered up the driveway, and the tenants, **gazing at the disgrace**, watched with heavy hearts.

2. The dog sat up, his mouth clenching the rolled newspaper, **wagging his tail**, and begged a reward.

3. The upholstered pieces, the expensive, polished tables had been moved into the huge dining room, **covered with endless painter's cloths so that they would be protected from the splatterings of paint**.

4. The meeting that had been like a marathon among meetings continued, and the leader deliberated about his strategy, **stalling after the last remarks from the representative with whom he had planned so many emergency ploys focusing upon every conceivable tactic for the suppression of the opposition**.

Practice 4 (page 21):

Part 1

1. With the core of the reel showing, his heart feeling stopped with excitement, **leaning back against the current that mounted icily up his thighs**, Nick thumbed the reel hard with his left hand.

2. Mrs. Carpenter was putting sun-tan oil on Sybil's shoulders, **spreading it down over the delicate, wing-like blades of her back**.

3. Soon the men began to gather, **surveying their own children, speaking of planting and rain, tractors and taxes**.

4. The *Carpathia* ship's passengers pitched in gallantly to help the survivors of the *Titanic*, providing extra toothbrushes, lending clothes, sewing smocks for the children out of steamer blankets brought along in the lifeboats.

Part 2

1. The children crawled over the shelves and into the potato and onion bins, **twanging all the time in their sharp voices like cigar-box guitars**.

2. He, **sensing a new and strange and quite terrified note in all this the moment he read it**, at once looked over his shoulder at her and, **seeing her face so white and drawn**, signaled that he would meet her.

3. In the late afternoon, the truck came back, **bumping** and **rattling through the dust**, and there was a layer of dust in the bed, and the hood was covered with dust, and the headlights were obscured with a red flour.

4. He stood there, **balancing on one leg** and **holding tightly to the edges of the window sill with his hands, staring at the sign and at the whitewashed lettering of the words**.

Putting the Participial Phrase to Work (page 22):
Answers will vary.

Skill 3
Absolute Phrase (page 24)

Practice 1 (page 26):
1. Then the rope tightened mercilessly while Buck struggled in fury, **his tongue lolling out of his mouth** and **his great chest panting**.

2. **His head aching, his throat sore**, he forgot to light the cigarette.

3. I looked across to a lighted case of Chinese design which held delicate-looking statues of horses and birds, small vases and bowls, **each set upon a carved wooden base**.

4. I was awake for quite a long time, thinking about things and watching Catherine sleeping, **the moonlight on her face**.

5. The dinosaur ran, **its pelvic bones crushing aside trees and bushes, its taloned feet clawing damp earth**, leaving prints six inches deep wherever it settled its weight.

6. She was now standing arms akimbo, **her shoulders drooping a little, her head cocked to one side, her glasses winking in the sunlight.**

7. And then, **his feet sinking in the soft nap of the carpet, his hand in one pocket clutching the money,** he felt as if he could squeal or laugh out loud.

8. Within, you could hear the signs and murmurs as the furthest chambers of it died, **the organs malfunctioning, liquids running a final instant from pocket to sac to spleen, everything shutting off,** closing up forever.

Practice 2 (page 28):

1. One customer in the line spoke out and ranted continuously about the unfair price, **the other customers rallying and demanding the same reduction in the cost.**

2. Several dancers near the band joined together and moved quickly into two lines, **one couple heading and leading the rest through the complicated steps.**

Practice 3 (page 29):

1. The youngest brother was nearby resting, **all his work over.**

2. As soon as it was over, they pranced around Gracie like courtiers, **Paul wooing her disgustingly with his stretched smiles.**

3. Later, so happy, he held the baby soothingly, and brought the music box to her and wound the toy up, **his voice singing with it.**

4. The student teacher erased everything quickly and, with a hurried cover-up, started to call out the spelling words for us, **her embarrassment definitely coming from her misspelling on the chalkboard.**

Practice 4 (page 31):

Part 1

1. Now, in the waning daylight, he turned into Glover Street toward his home, **his arms swinging as he moved onto the unpaved road.**

2. As they drove off Wilson saw her standing under the big tree, looking pretty rather than beautiful in her faintly rosy khaki, **her dark hair drawn back off her forehead and gathered in a knot low on her neck, her face as fresh, he thought, as though she were in England**.

3. His great chest was low to the ground, **his head forward and down, his feet flying like mad, the claws scarring the hard-packed snow in parallel grooves**.

4. In front of the house where we lived, the mountain went down steeply to the little plain along the lake, and we sat on the porch of the house in the sun and saw the winding of the road down the mountain-side and the terraced vineyards on the side of the lower mountain, **the vines all dead now for the winter and the fields divided by stone walls**, and below the vineyards, **the houses of the town on the narrow plain along the lake shore**.

Part 2

1. He began scrambling up the wooden pegs nailed to the side of the tree, **his back muscles working like a panther's**.

2. Touser roused himself under Fowler's desk and scratched another flea, **his leg thumping hard against the floor**.

3. They were smiling, **one woman talking, the others listening**.

4. Men, **their caps pulled down, their collars turned up**, swung by; a few women all muffled scurried along; and one tiny boy, **only his little black arms and legs showing out of a white wooly shawl**, was jerked along angrily between his father and mother; he looked like a baby fly that had fallen into the cream.

Putting the Absolute Phrase to Work (page 33):
Answers will vary.

Skill 4
Prepositional Phrase (page 34)

Practice 1 (page 36):

1. It was morning, and the new sun sparkled gold *across* **the ripples** *of* **a gentle sea.**

2. *With* **the flavor** *of* **ham and biscuit** *in* **his mouth,** the boy felt good.

3. *For* **the first fifteen years** *of* **our lives,** Danny and I lived *within* **five blocks** *of* **each other** and neither knew *of* **the other's existence.**

4. *At* **that moment,** a skinny arm shot out *between* **the bars** *of* **Wharton's cell** and grabbed Coffey's slab *of* **a bicep.**

5. *By* **the end** *of* **the first round,** his face felt as if it had been stung *by* **a hundred bees.**

6. *Over* **Dean's shoulder,** I could see the doctor *against* **the wall** *with* **his black bag** *between* **his feet.**

7. Ima Dean, *with* **a huge bag** *of* **yellow and red wrapped candies,** was sitting *on* **the floor,** delving *into* **it,** making one big pile and three smaller ones.

8. *With* **the ivy** *behind* **her,** *with* **the sunlight** *through* **the trees dappling her long blue cloak, and** *with* **her nice fresh face smiling** *across* **the greenery,** she was *like* **a** softly colored illustration *in* **one** *of* **Colin's books.**

Practice 2 (page 39):

1. The nature trail is a mile from the interstate, *near* **the canal by the old barn,** *near* **the historic museum in the 19th-century village, and** *near* **the old abandoned post office across from the church on Front Street.**

2. The first day of classes was chaos, *in* **the cafeteria with huge lines,** *in* **the guidance department with countless schedule changes, and** *in* **the main office with stressed-out administrators in high demand but low supply.**

Practice 3 (page 40):

1. *Under* the hood *of* the truck and *within* the interior *of* the cabin, there were wisps *of* smoke.

2. *After* the rain and wind *of* the most fierce hurricane, the crops drooped *toward* the soil, drying out *from* the sun.

3. *During* the ninth inning, Sherman caught a fly ball *in* the left field *near* the fence.

4. *On* the Internet, vast amounts *of* data traveled *with* the speed *of* invisible light, *with* clear resolution *of* graphics.

Practice 4 (page 42):

Part 1

1. *On* rocky islands, gulls woke.

2. Dad was a tall man *with* a large head, jowls, and a Herbert Hoover collar.

3. The crowd chased us *under* Louis XIV tables, *around* potted palms, *up* stairways, *around* corners, *down* stairways, *into* the main lobby.

4. Then he talked *of* other matters, *of* Shropshire, *of* schools and school life in general, *of* the news in that day's papers.

Part 2

5. *With* a final kick, a final marimba concert, a final autumnal lunge through leaf stacks, they went home.

6. The snow deadened his careful footsteps, *over* the smaller rocks, *over* the low thicket *of* leafless bushes.

7. He went the back way, *through* Deer's Pasture, *across* the schoolyard, and *around* the fence.

8. Then, *on* his back, *with* his tail lashing and his jaws clicking, the shark plowed *over* the water as a speedboat does.

Putting the Prepositional Phrase to Work (page 42):

1. A man stood *upon* **a railroad bridge** *in* **northern Alabama**, looking down *into* **the swift water** twenty feet below.

2. *About* **an hour** *before* **sunset**, *on* **the evening** *of* **a day** *in* **the beginning** *of* **October**, a man traveling *on* **foot** entered the little town *of* **D——**.

3. The boy *with* **fair hair** lowered himself *down* **the last few feet** *of* **rock** and began to pick his way *toward* **the lagoon**.

4. *In* **the ancient city** *of* **London**, *on* **a certain autumn day** *in* **the second quarter** *of* **the sixteenth century**, a boy was born *to* **a poor family** *of* **the name** *of* **Canty**. . . .

5. It was the best *of* **times**, it was the worst *of* **times**, it was the age *of* **wisdom**, it was the age *of* **foolishness**, it was the epoch *of* **belief**, it was the epoch *of* **incredulity**, it was the season *of* **light**, it was the season *of* **darkness**, it was the spring *of* **hope**, it was the winter *of* **despair**. . . .

Skill 5
Adjective Clause (page 44)

Practice 1 (page 46):

1. There was one fighter in those days, a pretty good light-heavyweight named Junior Ellis, *who* **used to sing along with country and western records before a bout**.

2. Little Jon, *whose* **eyes were quicker than most**, should have seen the hole, but all his attention was on the stars.

3. Boo had drifted to a corner of the room, *where* **he stood with his chin up**, peering from a distance at Jem.

4. The recent sudden death of Sir Charles Baskerville, *whose* **name has been mentioned as the probable liberal candidate for Mid-Devon at the next election**, has cast a gloom over the county.

5. We run bare-legged to the beach, **which lies smooth, flat and glistening with fresh wet shells after the night's tides**.

6. This leader, **whose word was law among boys who defied authority for the sake of defiance**, was no more than twelve or thirteen years old and looked even younger.

7. Thinking that his brother had run away with Christine, Philippe had dashed in pursuit of him along the Brussels Road, **where he knew that everything was prepared for the elopement**.

8. How strange it is that people of honest feeling and sensibility, **who would not take advantage of a man born without arms or legs or eyes**, think nothing of abusing a man born with low intelligence.

Practice 2 (page 48):

1. I closed the door, went outside, then greeted the mailman, **who was going down the street with his mailbag over his shoulder**, making his daily rounds.

2. The producer entered the theatre, took a seat, then watched the dancer, **who was rehearsing with only a piano for accompaniment**, learning the choreography.

Practice 3 (page 49):

1. Walking in his boots and sinking into the mud, the landscaper started to inspect the front and back of the garden, **where the downpour had washed away many of the new plants**.

2. While scrutinizing lovingly from the hallway, as if to rearrange all the china and flowers for the bridal party, she walked toward the dining table, **which was covered by a pure white lace tablecloth**.

3. Meredith perched in her apartment loft in the bohemian district, with Tramp, **who was a mutt**, and Lady, **who was a blue-ribbon pedigree**.

4. They had stopped to relax that afternoon at Berkley Springs, **which on most days was a very popular tourist site** and **where there was a famous spring-water well**.

Practice 4 (page 51):

1. Before Sheila left for America to be married two years before, she gave Ma a large and very beautiful volume of the complete works of Shakespeare, **which is now my dearest possession**.

2. His black hair, **which had been combed wet earlier in the day**, was dry now and blowing.

3. Percy had returned to the storage room, **where he probably felt more at ease on this particular night**.

4. The women, **who were never asked to do more than stay at home, cook food, and make clothing**, now must take the place of the men and face the dangers that abound beyond the village.

5. Mr. Sherlock Holmes, **who was usually very late in the mornings save upon those not infrequent occasions when he was up all night**, was seated at the breakfast table.

6. The terror, **which would not end for another twenty-eight years**, began, so far as I know or can tell, with a boat made from a sheet of newspaper floating down a gutter swollen with rain.

7. The taxi driver, **who had not yet been paid**, carefully placed Miss Hearne in the back seat of his car and started the engine.

8. One evening in late fall, George ran out of his house to the library, **where he hadn't been in years**.

Putting the Adjective Clause to Work (page 52):
Answers will vary.

Skill 6
Adverb Clause (page 54)

Practice 1 (page 56):

1. Susan, tears streaming, was out of the control room like a shot **when it was over**.

2. Finally he huddled by a fallen log, removed one boot, and rubbed his swollen ankle *while* **he gained his breath**.

3. ***When* he got back into town**, he would have to go on distributing his bundle of papers *before* **he went home to supper**.

4. ***When* the sun set**, he crouched by the path and cooked a small supper and listened to the fire crack *while* **he put the food in his mouth and chewed thoughtfully**.

5. ***When* kernel-picking time came**, *before* **it was dark each day**, the boy or the father took a hammer with a homemade handle, went to the flat rock, and cracked as many walnuts as could be kerneled in a night.

6. Her face, *as* **she stepped into the light**, was round and thick, and her eyes were like two immense eggs stuck into a white mess of bread dough.

7. ***When* the seal was dead**, the bear attended first to herself, getting rid of the wet from her coat *before* **it could freeze, *although* oil had kept off the frost so far**.

8. One autumn night, *when* **the first heavy rains were falling and a cold wind whistled through the valley**, a knock came at the minister's door, and opening it, he found an Indian boy, ragged, hungry, and footsore, who begged for food and shelter.

Practice 2 (page 59):

1. *After* **he jumped toward the edge of the rim**, he slam-dunked with his left hand, the best left hand in professional basketball.

2. *Although* **she had the fewest years of piano lessons among the contestants**, she walked away with the trophy for first place, a golden statue in the shape of a piano.

Practice 3 (page 59):

1. Tabitha's favorite activity, *after* **she started up her computer**, was on the Internet.

2. *After* **the beast's heart was transformed and in complete love with Belle**, he changed magically back into

the handsome prince of his past and in quick time dazzled everyone he greeted.

3. *Although* **the Barbie doll was almost legless from so much play**, Kylie used to walk her doll exclusively in the morning, *because* **her doll was just up from her night's sleep**.

4. In the game's last seconds after the winning pass to Brennan, *as* **the thunderous cheering rose to a gadzillion decibels**, his proud dad jumped up to sing the fight song of the team, the winners.

Practice 4 (page 61):

Part 1

1. *Before* **the girls got to the porch**, I heard their laughter crackling and popping like pine logs in a cooking stove.

2. *While* **the children stood half squabbling by the window**, their father leaned over a sofa in the adjoining room above a figure whose heart in sleep had quietly stopped its beating.

3. We had gone about ten miles *when* **Harry spotted a little turnout and veered the truck into it**.

4. My first impression, *as* **I opened the door**, was that a fire had broken out, *because* **the room was so filled with smoke that the light of the lamp upon the table was blurred by it**.

Part 2

5. *After* **he reached the little cleft where the road came through**, the afternoon wind struck him and blew up his hair and ruffled his shirt.

6. They were hateful sharks, bad smelling, scavengers as well as killers, and *when* **they were hungry, they would bite at an oar or the rudder of a boat**.

7. A child with a crooked mouth and twisted hands can very quickly and easily develop a set of very crooked and twisted attitudes both towards himself and life in general, especially *if* he is allowed to grow up with them without being helped to an understanding of them.

8. *When* she looked at the children and saw how tired they were, and *when* she thought of the number of trips they had made in past weeks, all to no purpose, to the East Parade Grounds, she decided that in spite of the instructions on the radio, she simply could not face starting out all over again.

Putting the Adverb Clause to Work (page 62):
Answers will vary.

Reviewing the Tools (page 66)

Practice 1 (page 66):

1a.	AP		11a.	PP
2a.	PREP		11b.	PREP
3a.	AP		12a.	PREP
4a.	AB		12b.	AB
5a.	AP		13a.	PP
6a.	ADJC		13b.	PREP
6b.	PREP		14a.	ADVC
7a.	AB		14b.	PREP
7b.	AB		15a.	PP
8a.	PP		15b.	PREP
8b.	PREP		16a.	PREP
9a.	P		16b.	AP
9b.	PREP		17a.	ADVC
10a.	ADVC		17b.	ADVC
10b.	PREP		18a.	PREP

18b.	PREP	26c.	PREP
18c.	PREP	26d.	ADVC
19a.	PREP	26e.	P
19b.	PREP	27a.	PREP
19c.	P	27b.	PREP
20a.	ADVC	27c.	P
20b.	ADJC	27d.	ADVC
20c.	PREP	28a.	PREP
21a.	AP	28b.	PREP
21b.	AP	28c.	PREP
21c.	ADJC	28d.	P
22a.	PREP	28e.	P
22b.	PREP	29a.	PREP
22c.	PREP	29b.	PREP
22d.	P	29c.	PREP
23a.	PREP	29d.	PREP
23b.	PREP	29e.	PREP
23c.	P	29f.	AB
23d.	ADJC	30a.	PP
24a.	PREP	30b.	PP
24b.	P	30c.	PP
24c.	P	30d.	PREP
24d.	P	30e.	PREP
25a.	PREP	30f.	P
25b.	PREP	30g.	P
25c.	PREP	30h.	P
25d.	PREP	30i.	P
26a.	PREP	30j.	P
26b.	ADVC	30k.	P

Practice 2 (page 70):
Answers will vary.

Skill 7
Sentence Opener Position (page 72)

Practice 1 (page 75):

1. On April 10, 1912, the *Titanic* left Southampton on her maiden voyage to New York.

2. **Without a word,** she took a piece of paper out of her pants pocket.

3. **Even then, when we might have kissed and embraced unrestrainedly**, our shyness prevented us from sharing anything but the most innocent pleasure.

4. **When people are young**, they desperately need to conform, and no one can embarrass a young person so much as an adult to whom he or she is related.

5. **When she came into the wings**, she was very upset and argued with the stage manager who, having seen me perform before Mother's friends, said something about letting me go on in her place.

6. **Being a star in her own right, earning twenty-five pounds a week**, she was well able to support herself and her children.

7. **Now, facing the bull,** he was conscious of many things at the same time.

8. **There, between two trees, against a background of gaunt black rocks**, was a figure from a dream, a strange beast that was horned and drunken-legged, but like something he had never even imagined.

Practice 2 (page 77):

1. **From the start, because the store had opened with haste,** Jackson worried constantly in dread during the day, wondering about his boss.

2. **At the dumpster, when the truck arrived with junk**, they emptied it out in minutes, piling up the garbage.

Practice 3 (page 78):
1. **After meeting with the president**, he signed and delivered the letter to the secretary.

2. **After she tried the choreography**, she met the director, and they planned to confer with the producer.

3. **Through all the ups and downs of the trial**, the lawyers and the judge, the defendant and the jury, had been intense listeners to the expert testimony.

4. **Too pleasant to fight with the customer about the return, and too aggreeable to resist**, Miss Simpson agreed with a smile, refunded the money without protest, and remained remarkably calm.

Practice 4 (page 80):
1. **When Hedger came slinking out of his closet**, he sat down on the edge of the couch, sat for hours without moving.

2. **When he was younger**, Murphy played halfback for Yale and was named to the All-East team.

3. **In her own mind**, the tall dark girl had been in those days much confused.

4. **When the night crept down in shadowy blue and silver**, they threaded the shimmering channel in the rowboat and, tying it to a jutting rock, began climbing the cliff together.

5. **On occasions when the tide ran exceptionally high**, waves washed perilously close to the lighthouse, dashing its base with salt-tinged algae, which clung to it now like sea moss.

6. **To a man so newly lonely, so newly alone**, an invitation out meant an evening in other people's lives, and therefore freedom from his own, and it meant the possibility of

laughter that would surprise him—how good it was to be alive and healthy, to have a body that had not given up in spite of everything.

7. **Whenever she lay awake beside her husband, like tonight**, she would still keep her eyes closed for a long time, then open them and relish with astonishment the blue of the brand-new curtains, replacing the apricot-pink which had filtered the morning light into the room where she had slept as a girl.

8. **By December of that year, more than twenty months after fleeing the house of Vess**, Ariel was eighteen years old, no longer a girl but a lovely young woman.

Putting the Sentence Opener Position to Work (page 81): Answers will vary.

Skill 8
Subject-Verb Split Position (page 83)

Practice 1 (page 86):
1. The writer, **an old man with a white mustache**, had some difficulty in getting into bed.

2. When Jesse Bentley, **absorbed in his own idea**, suddenly arose and advanced toward him, his terror grew until his whole body shook.

3. The twins, **smeary in the face, eating steadily from untidy paper sacks of sweets**, followed them in a detached way.

4. His hands, **beyond control**, ran up and down the soft-skinned baby body, the sinuous, limbless body.

5. Horace Whaley, **the Island County coroner**, swore softly on the courtroom Bible and edged into the witness box.

6. His face, **fresh from the pounding of Johnnie's fists**, felt more pleasure than pain in the wind and the driving snow.

7. The big hands, with the knotted, cracked joints and the square, horn-thick nails, hang loose off the wrist bone like clumsy, homemade tools hung on the wall of a shed after work.

8. The four pretty, slatternly Spanish girls, **their dark hair sleeked down over their ears, their thin-soled black slippers too short in the toes and badly run over at high heels**, took leisurely leave, with kisses all around, of a half dozen local young men, who had brought flowers and baskets of fruit.

Practice 2 (page 88):

1. In the flurry of traffic, the ambulance driver, **who only an hour ago had been asleep**, gripped the steering wheel, and his siren, **wailing like a giant in agony**, warned the traffic to make way.

2. Near the field of wheat, tough-skinned Jasper, **who a year ago had been an irresponsible drunk**, walked peacefully among his crops, and his serenity, **derived from his year's self-control with alcohol**, allowed him to concentrate on farming.

Practice 3 (page 89):

1. Nielsen Rating Service, **a determiner of TV ratings that had been accepted by the TV networks that season**, was surveying this morning.

2. The cook, **a fine-bellied gourmet**, was back in the kitchen at the closet freezer, ruminating about the latest beef selections, but the butcher reassured him.

3. Because the thunderstorm, **which was sudden and fierce in downpour**, brought to fields the rain for the crops and was steady enough to remain in the parched land and penetrate to the roots, the plants raised their branches and arched their stems toward the sun.

4. Janice Larson, **who successfully finished auto-mechanics, having been one of few girls in the course**, tried with great persistence for a related job and applied to

several employment agencies, where counselors were surprised at her sex, describing her prospects with guarded optimism but sincere hope.

Practice 4 (page 92):

1. When the match went out, the old man, **trembling from agitation**, peeped into the little window.

2. The country house, **on this particular wintry afternoon**, was most enjoyable.

3. At once Buntaro slid an arrow from the quiver and, **still sitting**, set up the bow, raised it, drew back the bowstring to eye level and released the shaft with savage, almost poetic liquidity.

4. These three trains, **motionless in the moonlight**, confirmed my fears that traffic was not maintained by night on this part of the line.

5. The first opportune minute came that very afternoon, and Cress, **after being warned**, went in tears to her room.

6. And my departure, which, **especially in my own eyes**, stank of betrayal, was my only means of proving, or redeeming, that love, my only hope.

7. Only a frying pan, **with an arrow through it**, remained.

8. His little dark eyes, **deepset under a tanned forehead**, and his mouth, **surrounded with wrinkles**, made him look attentive and studious.

Putting the Subject-Verb Split Position to Work (page 92):
Answers will vary.

Skill 9
Sentence Closer (page 95)

Practice 1 (page 98):

1. He went on, **limping**.

2. She was separated from Grandpa, **for what reason neither grand-parent would tell**.

3. It was a heavy sound, **hard and sharp, not rolling**.

4. And so we went to the station, across the meadow, **taking the longer way, trying to be together as long as possible**.

5. Sometimes a gaggle of them came to the store, **filling the whole room, chasing out the air and even changing the well-known scents**.

6. Hour after hour he stood there silent, **motionless, a shadow carved in ebony and moonlight**.

7. Prometheus was one of the Titans, **a gigantic race who inhabited the earth before the creation of man**.

8. Light flickered on bits of ruby glass and on sensitive capillary hairs in the nylon-brushed nostrils of the creature that quivered gently, gently, **its eight legs spidered under it on rubber-padded paws**.

Practice 2 (page 99):

1. They would meet, **deciding about their agenda for the sales meeting, their opinions uncertain, their interest high, the leader of the group of section chiefs shouting out like a huckster**.

2. She smiled, **glancing at the flowers in the vase, their stems poised, their blossoms in full bloom, the arrangement of the bouquet of roses looking like a prize-winner**.

Practice 3 (page 100):

1. High up the tree there climbed some girls, **little adventurers who imagined a great escapade of nearly Everest proportions**.

2. Inspecting the plumbing and fixtures that outfitted the new bathroom, he walked around, **his tappings and probings done with his expert skill, and his experience guiding his assessment of the work**.

3. They could foresee a time of soldiers ending their battles, and a period of permanent truce, **negotiating their disputes**

about politics, and many of the old arguments, living peacefully within dissent.

4. Then it was graduation, and they were encouraged by a dream of new beginnings for their lives, **marching among friends and proud parents, dressed in their caps and gowns as the orchestra, with brass fanfares, stirred them with its majesty of the pomp of trumpet blares and the circumstances of the formal rite of passage.**

Practice 4 (page 103):

1. She stood out from all the other girls in the school, **like someone with blue blood in her veins.**

2. His face was fleshy and pallid, **touched with colour only at the thick hanging lobes of his ears and at the wide wings of his nose.**

3. The young white man who served us did it in leisurely fashion, **with long pauses for a smoke.**

4. His earnestness affected the boy, **who presently became silent and a little alarmed.**

5. He was standing with her in the cold, **looking in through a grated window at a man making bottles in a roaring furnace.**

6. The girl at first did not return any of the kisses, but presently she began to, and after she had put several on his cheek, she reached his lips and remained there, **kissing him again and again as if she were trying to draw all the breath out of him.**

7. Mary Jane gazed after her, **a moody puzzled expression on her face, while Mrs. Conroy leaned over the banisters to listen for the hall-door.**

8. As far down the long stretch as he could see, the trout were rising, **making circles all down the surface of the water, as though it were starting to rain.**

Putting the Sentence Closer Position to Work (page 104):
Answers will vary.

Reviewing the Tools and Positions
(page 107)

Practice 1 (page 107):
1. POSITIONS: opener, closer
   (a) **Around the old gravestones (PREP)**,
       the grass was high,
   (b) **untended (PP)**.

2. POSITIONS: opener, closer
   (a) **As they swung on the turn (ADVC)**,
       the sled went over,
   (b) **spilling half its load through the loose lashings (P)**.

3. POSITIONS: opener, closer
   (a) **When she awoke several hours later (ADVC)**,
       Snow White saw the faces of seven bearded, vertically
       challenged men,
   (b) **surrounding the bed (P)**.

4. POSITIONS: subject-verb split, closer
   Fletcher Seagull,
   (a) **who loved aerobatics like no one else (ADJC)**,
       conquered his sixteen-point vertical slow roll and the
       next day topped it off with a triple cartwheel,
   (b) **his feathers flashing white sunlight to a beach
       from which more than one furtive eye watched
       (AB)**.

5. POSITIONS: opener, closer
   (a) **Subdued (PP)**,
       I fixed my attention upon Reverend Sykes,
   (b) **who seemed to be waiting for me to settle down
       (ADJC)**.

6. POSITIONS: opener, closer
   (a) **Wildly (ADV)**,
       Alfred bolted across the street,
   (b) **sidestepping a taxicab by inches (P)**,
   (c) **ignoring the horns and curses of braking drivers
       (P)**.

7. POSITIONS: opener, closer,
   (a) **In the far corner (PREP)**,
   the man was still asleep,
   (b) **snoring slightly on the intaking breath (P)**,
   (c) **his head back against the wall (AB)**.

8. POSITIONS: opener, closer,
   (a) **At night (PREP)**,
   she looked at the bright stars,
   (b) **sleeping little (P)**,
   (c) **listening to the river (P)**.

9. POSITIONS: subject-verb split, closer
   A big kitchen table,
   (a) **covered with one of those old-fashioned oilcloths (PP)**,
   was neatly set as if for a big party,
   (b) **with eight chairs (PREP)**,
   (c) **two on each side of the table (AB)**.

10. POSITIONS: opener, closer
    (a) **An excellent student (AP)**,
    Caroline received uniformly high grades,
    (b) **which she worked hard to get, (ADJC)**
    (c) **doing more than two hours of homework each day (P)**.

11. POSITIONS: opener, closer
    (a) **At the cemetery (PREP)**,
    my brothers and I buried Mother,
    (b) **taking our time speaking to her (P)**,
    (c) **as though she could hear us (ADVC)**.

12. POSITIONS: opener, closer
    (a) **His face lit by flames (AB)**,
    across the open hearth sat my father,
    (b) **leaning forward (P)**,
    (c) **his hands outspread to his knees (AB)**,
    (d) **his shoulders tense (AB)**.

13. POSITIONS: opener, closer
    (a) **Beyond the driver (PREP)**,
    (b) **beyond the windshield (PREP)**,

a structure appeared,
(c) **indistinct (ADJ)**,
(d) **unidentifiable (ADJ)**.

14. POSITIONS: opener, closer
    (a) **Across the tops (PREP)**,
    (b) **of about a hundred gravestones and many people (PREP)**,
    I saw Viola in her black dress,
    (c) **standing on a little rise (P)**,
    (d) **her gray hair wandering from its knot (AB)**.

15. POSITIONS: opener, closer
    (a) **In an upstairs bedroom (PREP)**,
    (b) **shortly (ADV)**
    (c) before dawn **(PREP)**,
    a young American mother sat on the edge of a steel-framed bed,
    (d) **rocking her nursing daughter (P)**.

16. POSITIONS: opener, closer
    (a) **Periodically (ADV)**,
    wheelchair vans or ambulances or private cars parked in front of the portico and new residents were escorted in.
    (b) **a few on their own feet (AB)**,
    (c) **others in wheelchairs (AB)**,
    (d) **some on gurneys (AB)**.

17. POSITIONS: opener, closer
    (a) **Outside the window (PREP)**,
    Roland has stopped chopping and is sitting on the chopping block,
    (b) **his arms on his knees (AB)**,
    (c) **his big hands dangling (AB)**,
    (d) **staring off into the trees (P)**.

18. POSITIONS: opener, closer
    (a) **On the last, cold day (PREP)**,
    (b) **of December (PREP)**,
    (c) **in the year 406 (PREP)**,
    the river Rhine froze solid,
    (d) **providing the natural bridge the hundreds of**

thousands of hungry men, women, and children had been waiting for.

19. POSITIONS: opener, closer
    (a) **At the university (PREP)**,
    (b) **in his gray suit (PREP)**,
    he had seemed of no more than medium height,
    (c) **perhaps because he stooped so attentively to hear the slightest word from the person he was talking to (ADVC)**,
    (d) **perhaps because his neat, fair hair made him look somehow ineffectual (ADVC)**.

20. POSITIONS: opener, closer
    (a) **At three forty-five (PREP)**,
    he came up to the house again and said good-bye to the children,
    (b) **who were seated on the porch (ADJC)**,
    (c) **drinking apple juice(P) and**
    (d) eating graham crackers **(P)** and
    (e) **rolling pebbles back and forth (P)**.

21. POSITIONS: opener, subject-verb split
    (a) **After rain (PREP)**, or
    (b) **when snowfalls thaw (ADVC)**, the streets,
    (c) **unnamed (PP)**,
    (d) **unshaded (PP)**,
    (e) **unpaved (PP)**,
    turn from the thickest dust into the direst mud.

22. POSITIONS: opener, closer
    (a) **Shifting the weight of the line to his shoulder (P)** and
    (b) **kneeling carefully (P)** he washed his hand in the ocean and held it there for more than a minute,
    (c) **submerged (PP)**,
    (d) **watching the blood trail away and the steady movement of the water against his hand (P)**
    (e) **as the boat moved (ADVC)**.

23. POSITIONS: opener, closer
    (a) **On occasions (PREP)**
    (b) **when the tide ran exceptionally high (ADVC)**,

waves washed perilously close to the lighthouse,
(c) **dashing its base (P)**
(d) **with salt-tinged algae (PREP)**,
(e) **which clung to it now like a sea moss (ADJC)**.

24. POSITIONS: opener, closer
   (a) **Turning (P)**
   (b) **his shoulder pressing against the wall (AB)**,
      he moved
   (c) **until he was standing sideways (ADVC)**,
   (d) **his feet together on the narrow ledge (AB)**,
   (e) **his side hugging the wall (AB)**,
   (f) **as he faced the wide opening (ADVC)**.

25. POSITIONS: opener, closer
   (a) **Blindly (ADV)**, his right hand flew over the ledge,
   (b) **his fingers dancing across it (AB)**,
   (c) **reaching (P)**,
   (d) **feeling (P)**,
   (e) **searching (P)**,
   (f) until his body began to drop **(ADVC)**.

26. POSITIONS: opener, subject-verb split
   (a) **In the morning (PREP)**,
   (b) **breakfastless (ADJ)**,
      and
   (c) **shaky (ADJ)**,
   (d) **from seven cups (PREP)**,
   (e) **of coffee (PREP)**,
      Quoyle,
   (f) **heart and stomach aching (AB)**,
      went to the wharf on his way to Wavey.

27. POSITIONS: opener, closer
   (a) **Through the thicket (PREP)**,
   (b) **across the river (PREP)**,
      and
   (c) **in the deep, deep woods (PREP)**,
      lived a family of bears,
   (d) **a Papa bear (AP)**,
   (e) **a Mama Bear (AP)**,
      and

(f) **a Baby Bear (AP)**,

(g) **who all lived together anthropomorphically in a little cottage as a nuclear family (ADJC)**.

28. POSITIONS: opener, closer

(a) **When Laurel was a child (ADVC)**,
     she was sent to sleep

(b) **by the beloved reading voice (PREP)**,

(c) **under a velvety cloak (PREP)**,

(d) **of words (PREP)**,

(e) **patterned richly (PP)**,
     and

(f) **stitched with gold (PP)**,

(g) **coming straight out (P)**,

(h) **of a fairy tale (PREP)**,

(i) **while the voice went on reading aloud into her dreams (ADVC)**.

29. POSITIONS: subject-verb split, closer

The sun,

(a) **red (ADJ)**
     and

(b) **enormous (ADJ)**,
     began to sink

(c) **into the western sky (PREP)**,

(d) **the moon beginning to rise (AB)**,

(e) **on the other side (PREP)**,

(f) **of the river (PREP)**,

(g) **with its own glorious shade (PREP)**,

(h) **of red (PREP)**,

(i) **coming up out of the trees like a russet firebird (P)**.

30. POSITIONS: opener, closer

(a) **In the half-light (PREP)**,
     my eyes roamed,

(b) **around my room (PREP)**,

(c) **a cramped space (AP)**,

(d) **the room of an only child (AP)**,

(e) **tidy (ADJ)**,

(f) **organized completely (PP)**,

(g) **with the possessory feel (PREP)**,

(h) **of everything (PREP)**,

(i) **in place (PREP)**,

(j) **unmolested by any of the brothers and sisters I had for years longed to have and now, in my desolation, longed for with a special ache (PP)**.

The Last Practice (page 115):

Answers will vary.